D1371046

QUALITY MATTERS

Excellence in Early Childhood Programs

ADDISON-WESLEY EARLY CHILDHOOD EDUCATION

QUALITY MATTERS

Excellence in Early Childhood Programs

Gillian Doherty-Derkowski

Addison-Wesley Publishers Limited

Don Mills, Ontario • Reading, Massachusetts
Menlo Park, California • New York • Wokingham, England
Amsterdam • Bonn • Sydney • Singapore • Tokyo
Madrid • San Juan

Canadian Cataloguing in Publication Data

Doherty, Gillian, 1938-
    Quality matters: excellence in early childhood programs

(Addison-Wesley early childhood education)
Rev. ed. of: Quality matters in child care.
Includes bibliographical references and index.
ISBN 0-201-76614-0

I.   Child care services - Evaluation. I. Title.
II.   Title: Quality matters in child care.
III.   Series.

HV851.D65 1994   362.7'12   C94-931740-3

Printed and bound in Canada by Webcom

ISBN 0-201-76614-0

A B C D E WC 99 98 97 96 95

Contents

◆ ◆ ◆ ◆ Preface

The first six years of life have long been considered crucial for the child's later development. Hence, we have sayings such as: "Give me the first six years of a child's life and you can have the rest," and "As the twig is bent, so grows the tree." Research in developmental psychology supports the notion that what happens in the first six years of life is crucial. This book takes a detailed look at the behaviors of the adults, and the characteristics of the early childhood program, that have a positive or negative effect on the young child's well-being and development.

This book is written with the firm conviction that:

◆ desirable adult behavior with and towards young children is much more likely to occur if adults understand the implications of what they are doing; and

◆ research findings can, and should, be used as the foundation for determining desirable practice.

There are two major themes in this book, namely:

◆ the uniqueness of each child; and

◆ the importance of what goes on between the adult and the child on a daily basis.

Chapter 1 serves as an introduction. It defines the term "quality", presents five different ways of looking at quality, and discusses why we should be concerned about quality in early childhood programs. The second chapter reviews the major research findings regarding the relationship between child well-being and/or development and the overall quality of an early childhood program. The major theme of the importance of what goes on between the child and adult on a daily basis is explored in detail in Chapters 3 and 4. Chapter 5 discusses the research findings related to other important aspects of the child's daily experience, namely: parent involvement, staff consistency, programming, and the physical environment. Chapter 6 examines the impact of differences in the so-called "structural" features of a program, for example, the number of children for whom an adult is responsible. Chapter 7 looks at the adult work environment and discusses how it impacts on the child. The influence of factors outside the program, such as the strictness of state, provincial, or territorial regulations, is discussed in Chapter 8. Chapter 9 examines various mechanisms for obtaining and maintaining quality. The following chapter explores the special issues associated with providing a quality early childhood program in a multicultural society. Chapter 11 discusses the issues associated with providing a quality early childhood program for children with special needs. Chapter 12 provides a basic description of how research is done, and identifies some of the methodological challenges faced by researchers. This chapter could be read after Chapter 1, in order to provide a background for considering the research discussed. The final chapter identifies three important emerging issues in the early childhood field.

Within the text, a new term is introduced in **bold** typeface and defined at that point. A glossary of the most important terms is provided immediately following the text, before the list of references. The extensive list of references can be used to identify the location of reports cited in the text, and to identify people who are working in a particular area and who may have published material subsequent to the document review done for this book. An index follows the list of references.

The research studies cited or discussed in this book were all conducted in settings receiving the usual level of resources for their jurisdiction. Findings from studies conducted in such settings can, therefore, be used to inform practice in ordinary programs. Because we know that family background influences child development, only studies that compared children with similar backgrounds, or controlled for differences through a statistical procedure, were used.

When reading this book, it should be assumed that the difference in research findings related to children in high quality settings versus low quality settings was significant at the .05 level or better. Significance at the .05 level or better means that the probability of the relationship having occurred by chance is less than 5 in 100. Within the scientific community, this level of significance indicates the relationship is the result of the variable being studied, for example, staff education. Results from studies where differences in programs were found, but not at the above level of significance, are reported as trends. This is indicated by a phrase such as: "There was a trend for children in programs with ..... to show ....."

◆ ◆ ◆ ◆ Acknowledgments

The initial literature review upon which this book is based was undertaken in 1990 as part of a project funded by the Ontario Ministry of Community and Social Services. The Ministry's permission to use this material is gratefully acknowledged. A second search to update the material was conducted in December, 1993. Barbara Dillon and Chris Gehman of the Childcare Resource and Research Unit at the University of Toronto provided much appreciated assistance in locating and obtaining documents. Throughout the writing of this book, my husband, Andrzej Derkowski, distributed large doses of moral support and encouragement. Finally, a sincere thank you to the people who reviewed the initial manuscript and provided many useful comments. They were Karen Chandler, Gyda Chud, Elaine Frankel, Kenise Murphy Kilbride, Steve Musson, and Connie Winder. Their input definitely made this a better book.

1 Introduction

In this book, the term **early childhood program** refers to a variety of programs for children below the age of six, namely: nursery school (sometimes called preschool), child care, and both junior and senior kindergarten. These early childhood programs were originally established for different reasons:

◆ *child care* programs were originally intended simply to provide basic care and supervision for children while their parents were at work;

◆ *nursery schools* were usually established to provide enrichment experiences for children and, therefore, emphasized creative play and social skill development; and

◆ *kindergartens* for five-year-olds were originally viewed as an opportunity to prepare the child for entry into the formal school system. Therefore, historically, they emphasized the development of school-related skills, such as sitting quietly and following the teacher's instructions.

The different original purposes of child care, nursery school, and kindergarten were associated with different philosophies about, and different approaches to, working with children. Not surprisingly, the different programs also had, and in fact continue to have, different educational requirements for the staff working in them.

Over the past twenty years, there has been an increasing number of child care programs and nursery schools operating in buildings that also house kindergarten programs. More frequent contact, and a shared concern for the well-being and development of young children, have encouraged the sharing of ideas and approaches among people working in different types of early childhood programs. There has also been a growing recognition that children of a given age have the same needs regardless of the type of early childhood program they attend.

Types of Early Childhood Programs

Kindergarten programs

The term "kindergarten" refers to a school-based group program, staffed by teachers, that serves either four- or five-year-olds (junior and senior kindergarten respectively). Generally the program is part-day, that is, morning or afternoon only.

Child care programs

The term "child care" includes nursery school and a variety of other types of care that involve children age 0 to 12. In North America, child care takes the following forms:

◆ full-time or part-time group programs outside a home setting. The children are often grouped in different rooms on the basis of age, as follows: infants (birth to around age 18 months), toddlers (roughly age 18 months to three years), preschoolers (age two-and-a-half or three years to six years), and school-aged. Depending on where they operate, these programs may be referred to as child care centers, day care centers, or early childhood centers;

◆ nursery schools. These are part-time group programs outside a home setting that generally target three-, four-, and five-year-olds;

◆ specialized part-time group programs outside a home setting for children attending school and with a specific mandate to provide care outside school hours. These so-called **school-age programs** involve children from kindergarten to age 12. They may operate before and/or after school, during lunch time, and/or during school holidays;

◆ care by a non-relative in that person's own home (**home-based child care**). This almost inevitably involves a mixed-age group, for example, an infant, two toddlers, and a preschooler; and

◆ care by a non-relative in the child's own home, for example, care provided by a mother's helper or a nanny.

Consistencies

There is a significant overlap in the functioning of nursery school, kindergarten, and child care programs. All involve an element of "care", for example, assisting children to take off and put on coats and boots. All high quality programs involve an element of "education", that is, they deliberately provide activities to assist the child's skill development. Furthermore, there are now enough research studies to enable us to confidently identify both the adult behaviors and the program characteristics associated with positive outcomes for children. These behaviors and program characteristics are the same across all types of early childhood programs. The following chapters discuss these research findings in greater detail and their implications for practice.

The Concept of Quality

Definition

The term "high quality" suggests something that is desirable or meets more than minimal standards. For parents thinking of enrolling their child in an early childhood program, the first concerns are the child's health and safety. These preoccupations reflect the reality that young children's physical well-being is highly dependent on the adults in their environment. Parents are only able to consider other aspects of the program when they are comfortable that the child's health and safety will be assured. However, a program that only addresses health and safety is simply **custodial**. In other words, it is not designed to promote or encourage the development of the child's skills.

Early childhood educators look at the quality of a program in terms of its effect on *both* the child's well-being and the child's development. They also consider whether or not the program supports and complements the family in its child-rearing role. Therefore, early childhood educators define **high quality** early childhood programs as follows:

A high quality early childhood program is one that:

◆ *supports and assists the child's physical, emotional, social, language, and intellectual development; and*

◆ *supports and complements the family in its child-rearing role.*

Different perspectives on quality

Katz (1993) suggests that the following five different perspectives should all be considered when determining the quality of a program:

◆ the *top-down perspective*, that is, examination of easily observed and measured program characteristics, for example, the number of children for whom each adult is responsible (known as the **staff-to-child ratio**) and staff qualifications. These program characteristics set the stage for quality programing to occur or not occur;

◆ the *bottom-up perspective*, that is, the quality of life experienced by the child in the program on a day-to-day basis;

◆ the *inside perspective*, that is, the working conditions experienced by staff members;

◆ the *outside-inside perspective*, that is, the relationship between staff member and parent; and

◆ the *outside perspective*, that is, the relationship between the program and the community in which it operates and society at large.

As will become evident in later chapters, research supports the concept of quality being multi-dimensional and involving all the five perspectives suggested by Katz.

The top-down perspective

Research has demonstrated **a statistically significant relationship**[1] between child development and early childhood program characteristics such as: the staff-to-child ratio, staff training in child development and early childhood education, and group size. For example, children in programs where staff have training in early childhood education have higher developmental levels than same-aged children in programs where staff lack such training. The studies that have looked at quality from a top-down perspective, and the implications for practice of their findings, are discussed in Chapter 6.

The bottom-up perspective

Katz suggests that the lasting effects of a program depend primarily on how it is experienced by the children participating in it. Looking at quality from this perspective requires making inferences about how each child would answer questions such as the following.

- Do I usually feel in this program that I am someone who is recognized as an individual, not someone who is just part of the crowd?

- Do I usually feel accepted, understood, and protected by the adults, rather than scolded or neglected by them?

- Am I usually treated and addressed seriously and respectfully by the adults, rather than treated as someone who is cute?

- Do I find most of the activities engaging, absorbing, and challenging, rather than frivolous, mindless, or boring?

- Do I find most of my experiences satisfying, rather than frustrating or confusing?

- Am I usually glad to be here, rather than reluctant to come and eager to leave?

The above questions emphasize the importance of the child feeling welcomed and comfortable in the program and also feeling intellectually engaged and respected. High quality early childhood programs involve more than simply keeping the children safe, happy, and busy.

The use of the qualifier "usually" not only recognizes that both children and programs have "off" days, so that the inferred answers should reflect experiences over a period of time, but also emphasizes the impact of repetition. Experiences may be benign or of little consequence if they are rare, but they will be either beneficial or harmful if they are frequent. For example, occasional experiences of the adult not paying attention to the child should not have a lasting impact. However, research studies have shown a statistically significant relationship between repeated adult lack of involvement with the children in early childhood programs and delayed social and language development in the children.

Research studies which have examined quality from the bottom-up perspective, and the implications for practice of their findings, are discussed in Chapters 3, 4, and 5.

The inside perspective

This perspective considers how the program is experienced by the people who work in it. Research in the United States has found that the way in which the administration treats the staff has an impact on how staff members feel about the early childhood program and their general level of job satisfaction. Low levels of job satisfaction, in turn, predict high **staff turnover rates** (levels of leaving the program). Several studies have found a statistically significant relationship between high staff turnover rates in early childhood programs and negative child outcomes. Chapter 7 examines the impact of the adult work environment (or what Katz calls the inside perspective) on program quality.

The outside-inside perspective

This perspective considers the relationship between the program staff member and the child's parent. Katz views this as ideally involving:

◆ frequent contacts;

◆ the exchange of meaningful information; and

◆ a relationship that is respectful and accepting of the parent rather than patronizing or rejecting.

Both Cloutier (1985), a Canadian, and Powell (1989), from the United States, have pointed out that families and early childhood programs constitute different social environments. The environments differ in terms of childrearing values, the types of behavior expected from the child, and the patterns of interaction between adults and children. Therefore, regular, frank communication between the parent and the early childhood program is important to increase the consistency of approach with the child across the two settings. This is particularly crucial around certain developmental tasks such as toilet training and learning to dress. Research findings related to parent involvement and the importance of involving the child's family are discussed in Chapters 5, 10, and 11.

The outside perspective

The fifth perspective, that is the relationship between the program and both the community in which it operates and society at large, introduces the concepts of:

- the program's responsibility to the children it serves and their families, and to the community, for the quality of the program and the way in which public funds are used. This responsibility includes respecting and addressing cultural differences and differences in abilities, as discussed in Chapters 10 and 11; and

- society's obligation to make decisions and adopt policies that encourage rather than jeopardize children's development. We all reap the benefits to be derived from high quality early childhood programs that assist children in developing the skills they need for a productive life. Similarly, we all suffer social and other costs as a result of the negative impact of poor quality early childhood programs on children's development.

The Importance of Quality

There are several reasons why we need to be concerned about the level of quality in early childhood programs. These reasons include:

- the clear evidence we now have that the first six years of life are crucial for the development of the basic interpersonal, language, and intellectual skills that will determine adult competence;

- the number of children under age six receiving non-relative care on a regular basis for at least part of the day;

- the proven negative impact of poor quality early childhood programs on children's well-being and development; and

- the apparent inability of a two-parent, middle-class home to compensate for the impact of poor quality early childhood programs.

The first six years of life

Interpersonal relationship skills

A child's peer relationship skills predict adult ability to function successfully with others. In order to function appropriately in a peer group, the child must master a number of social skills by age six. These include: how to initiate social contact with a peer, how to share and take turns, how to resolve conflict without resorting to aggression, and how to "read" non-verbal social communication. Children who have not developed adequate social skills by age six are likely to be rejected by their peers in elementary school (Howes, 1987).

Research from the United States has found that a child's status as popular with other children or rejected by them in the early grades of elementary school tends to persist throughout elementary school (Coie & Dodge, 1983; Coie & Kupersmidt, 1983; Dodge, 1983). Rejected children have limited opportunities to gain the social skills they lack when they are in elementary school because the other children refuse to play with them. Two American studies which followed the same children for several years found a statistically significant relationship between peer rejection in elementary school and the likelihood of later delinquency and school drop-out (Cowen et al., 1973; Parker & Asher, 1987). As discussed in later chapters, research has found a direct link between the quality of the early childhood program received by the child and the child's level of interpersonal relationship skills.

Language skills

Research conducted in the United States, in England, and in Bermuda comparing same-age preschool children has found a statistically significant relationship between:

◆ language fluency and vocabulary; and

◆ the extent of the preschool child's exposure to language and to opportunities for two-way communication.

Preschool children who lack adequate opportunities to hear and use language do not develop either the ability to express themselves or the listening and understanding skills expected for their age. Studies on the acquisition of a second language or sign language by children of different ages suggest that there may be a critical period before age seven during which language is learned most readily. These studies also demonstrate that children's language fluency during this critical period may determine their language fluency in adulthood (Johnson & Newport, 1989; Newport, 1988). Whether or not there is a critical period, the child who enters elementary school with listening and expressive skills below age-expectation will be less able than other children to take advantage of the learning opportunities provided. As discussed in later chapters, children enrolled in poor quality early childhood programs have been found to have poorer language skills than their counterparts enrolled in good quality programs.

Intellectual skills

Studies conducted in the United States and Canada have found a decline in intellectual functioning starting with a sudden decrease at age 18 to 24 months and continuing throughout the preschool period among children from families with a very low **socioeconomic status** (Belsky & Steinberg, 1978; Burchinal et al., 1989; Ramey & Haskins, 1981; Wright, 1983). Socioeconomic status refers to the family's degree of advantage as measured by a combination of factors such as the family income and the parents' level of education. Children from families with very low socioeconomic status are sometimes referred to as being **at environmental risk**.

It should be noted that the above research did not find that children from lower socioeconomic backgrounds started life with lower intellectual potential. The decline in intellectual functioning starting around 18 months is believed to result from lack of language stimulation and opportunities to play with a variety of materials during the toddler and preschool years. Support for this belief comes from the large body of research that has demonstrated that high quality early childhood programs prevent intellectual decline in children from very low socioeconomic backgrounds (for example, Burchinal et al., 1989; Berrueta-Clement et al., 1985; Lazar & Darlington, 1982; Wright, 1983). As will be discussed later in this chapter, middle-class children enrolled in early childhood programs that do not provide adequate stimulation have been found to have lower language and intellectual skills than same-age middle-class children enrolled in high quality programs.

Children under age six receiving non-relative care on a regular basis

As recently as 25 years ago, the idea of a preschool-age child being regularly looked after by someone other than the parent or a relative was unacceptable to many people in North America. However, the failure of wages to keep pace with inflation, plus increased taxes, has resulted in a real decline in the average family's purchasing power. This has made it necessary for many mothers to enter the paid workforce. At the same time, the extent to which family members live near each other has decreased, making grandparents less available to look after their grandchildren. The following statistics for both the United States and Canada illustrate the significant number of children under age six known to be or likely to be receiving regular non-relative care on at least a part-time basis.

According to Health and Welfare Canada (1994), in *Canada*, in 1992, there were:

♦ 720,635 children under age six with both parents working full-time, with one parent working full-time and the other a full-time student, or who had only one parent and that parent worked full-time or was a full-time student; and

♦ an additional 215,257 children under age six with both parents working or studying part-time for at least 20 hours a week, or who had only one parent and that parent worked or studied part-time for at least 20 hours a week.

It is reasonable to assume that most of these children are receiving regular non-relative care on at least a part-time basis.

Hofferth et al. (1991), of the Urban Institute in Washington, D.C., estimated that in the *United States* in 1990, 13.5 million children under age six were receiving regular care from someone other than a parent or relative. Of these, an estimated close to 12 million children had a mother in the paid workforce.

The impact of poor quality programs

The overall impact of poor quality early childhood programs is best illustrated by longitudinal research using a global perspective. **Longitudinal research** observes the same settings and/or individuals at two or more points in time, for example, the same children when they are age three and age seven. Studies examining programs from a **global** perspective look at a number of different characteristics of the program at the same time rather than focusing on only one characteristic of it.

Longitudinal research using a global perspective on quality has found a statistically significant relationship between *poor* quality early childhood programs and children who, in *elementary* school:

◆ are rated as having more behavior problems than peers who had been enrolled in high quality early childhood programs prior to entering grade one (Howes, 1988; Vandell et al., 1988; Vandell & Corasaniti, 1990);

◆ have poorer social skills with peers and are less accepted by them (Vandell et al., 1988; Vandell & Corasaniti, 1990);

◆ show poorer academic progress relative to their apparent ability than do children who were in high quality programs (Howes, 1988; Vandell & Corasaniti, 1990); and

◆ are rated by teachers as being less independent (Jacobs et al., 1992).

It is significant to note that the effect of poor quality early childhood programs was demonstrated to be still apparent in eight-year-olds by Vandell et al. (1988) and by Vandell & Corasaniti (1990).

The inability of the home to compensate for poor quality

Research indicates that a two-parent, middle-class family, with parents who have a high school or higher level of education, may not be able to compensate for the negative impact of a poor quality early childhood program, at least not for children in full-time attendance.

In a study conducted in the United States involving middle-class three- to five-year-olds, the children in *poor quality* programs showed significantly poorer language skills than the children in high quality programs (Peterson & Peterson, 1986). There were no significant differences between the two groups of children on parent education level, a family factor known to influence children's language skills.

Howes (1990), also in the United States, conducted a study that involved middle-class children, 85 percent of whom had both parents living at home. She found that the quality of the child care that the child had experienced accounted for between 7 percent and 22 percent of the differences observed in children's behaviors in kindergarten among children who had been enrolled in child care as infants. In comparison, the interaction between the child and the parent accounted for only 5 percent of the differences in behavior. When in kindergarten, children who had been in *poor quality* child care had more difficulty with peers, were less obedient with adults, and were rated by teachers as being more distractible, more hostile, and less able to remain focused on a task than children who had been in high quality programs.

In a third American study, Vandell et al. (1988) found that middle-class children who had been in *poor quality* child care had poorer social skills and were less accepted by their peers at age eight than comparable children who had been in good quality child care.

Melhuish et al. (1990a; 1990b) studied a group of home-based child care settings and a group of child care centers in England. The physical environment in most of the centers was rated as being poorer than in most of the home-based settings. In addition, the center staff members were rated by the researchers as providing less stimulation for the children than did the home-based child care providers. In spite of the fact that the children in the centers were "markedly the most advantaged group in terms of income, occupational status, and mother's education" (page 863), their language skills were at a lower developmental level than those of age-mates in home-based child care.

The finding that the home environment may not be able to compensate for a poor quality early childhood program should not be surprising. Children in full-time attendance spend a significant number of their waking hours in the program. If enrolled as infants, they spend more of their waking hours in the program than they do with their parents.

Implications for Practice

What happens to children during their first six years of life is crucial for the development of their basic social, language, and intellectual skills and for their future competence. A significant number of children are enrolled in early childhood programs, and we know that poor quality programs have a negative impact on children's well-being and development. It also appears that a middle-class, two-parent home may not be able to compensate for the negative impact of poor quality early childhood programs, at least not for children in full-time attendance. Therefore, we have to be concerned about the quality of early childhood programs.

What is required for quality in an early childhood program has been examined by research conducted in Canada, the United States, Bermuda, England, the Netherlands, New Zealand, and Sweden. These studies, as a group, have demonstrated that high quality early childhood programs require:

◆ **health and safety provisions** that ensure the children's well-being;

◆ **a physical and administrative environment** that enhances the program for children and staff alike;

◆ **staff-to-child ratios** that enable frequent personal interactions between each child and staff member;

◆ **group sizes** that allow children's interactions with other children and adults in the program to be personal and individual;

◆ adults who have **specific training in child development and early childhood education**. This increases the likelihood that the program will encourage the child's development and that the adult's interactions with the child are appropriate for the child's age, responsive to the child's needs, and are warm;

◆ **staffing that is stable** so that children have a chance to develop a trust relationship with the adult; and

◆ **programming** that is appropriate for the child's developmental level and recognizes individual differences.

The research supporting the above list of what is required, and the resultant implications for practice, is discussed in Chapters 3 to 7, 10, and 11.

Notes

[1] Statistically significant is a statistical term. It is used to signify that, on the basis of a statistical analysis, the apparent relationship between two items, for example, the staff-to-child ratio and the level of children's language skills, could not have happened simply by chance.

Quality from a Global Perspective

The impact of early childhood programs on children has been studied from both:

◆ a **discrete** perspective, that is, by focusing on the impact of only one characteristic of a program. For example, a researcher might study the impact of a certain type of adult behavior on children's language development; and

◆ a global perspective, that is, by focusing on the impact of a number of different characteristics of the program at the same time. For example, a researcher might study the impact on children's social skill development of both the percentage of staff with a college diploma and the number of children per staff member. In this situation, the two program characteristics would be combined to form one **composite** measure.

Studies using the *discrete* perspective on quality in early childhood programs enable us to know precisely which adult behaviors and which program characteristics have a statistically significant relationship with child well-being and development. This information, in turn, provides guidance for preferred practice. Studies which were conducted using a discrete perspective are discussed in Chapters 3 to 7.

Consistent with the observation made in Chapter 1 that quality is multi-dimensional, it is also useful to be aware of the findings from research that took a *global* perspective. These studies are the subject of this chapter.

Studies using a global perspective begin by classifying the subject programs as either high or low quality. This is done by either:

- the development of a composite measure of quality for each program in the study through assigning scores to a number of program characteristics in order to come up with an overall score. The most common characteristics used for this purpose are: the number of children per adult (known as the staff-to-child ratio), staff training, and the number of children per classroom; or

- the use of an observational rating scale that provides scores for a number of different characteristics of the program as well as a total score for it. One example is the *Early Childhood Environment Rating Scale* (Harms & Clifford, 1980), which is often referred to as the ECERS. This is used in center-based programs. Another is the *Family Day Care Rating Scale* (Harms & Clifford, 1989). This is used for home-based child care settings and abbreviated as the FDCRS.

Both the above approaches were developed by people who had been working in early childhood programs for a number of years. As a result of their observations and experience, they had come to believe that certain program characteristics were related to child well-being and optimal development. Subsequent research has confirmed their beliefs.

Research studies can be either:

- **concurrent,** that is, they examine the impact of the program on the children while the children are still enrolled in it; or

- **longitudinal,** that is, they observe the same settings and/or individuals at two or more different points in time.

The research using a global perspective discussed in this chapter includes both concurrent and longitudinal studies.

When examining the findings of any research study, it is important to remember that the researcher will only find information pertaining to the outcome studied. For example, a researcher who measures outcome solely on the basis of social skills cannot report on the impact of the program on other areas of development. Situations where information about the impact of a program on a particular type of development was sought, and the program's quality rating had no apparent effect, are identified. This will enable the reader to know when the failure to report a relationship does not simply indicate that the particular type of outcome was not examined.

Concurrent Research

Concurrent studies using a global perspective on quality in early childhood programs have demonstrated the positive impact on children of being in a program classified as high quality in:

◆ Canada (Goelman & Pence, 1988; Schliecker et al., 1991; White et al., 1988);

◆ the United States (Howes & Olenick, 1986; Howes & Stewart, 1987; Kontos & Fiene, 1986; Kontos & Fiene, 1987; Peterson & Peterson, 1986; Vandell & Powers, 1983);

◆ Bermuda (Phillips et al., 1987); and

◆ England (Melhuish et al., 1990a, 1990b).

The Goelman & Pence and the Howes & Stewart studies looked at home-based child care while Melhuish et al. examined both home-based and center-based child care. The other studies examined center-based or kindergarten programs only.

The studies as a group demonstrate that programs classified as high quality are associated with children who, in comparison with peers who are in programs classified as low quality:

◆ have higher levels of language development (Goelman & Pence, 1988; Melhuish et al., 1990a, 1990b; Peterson & Peterson, 1986; Phillips et al., 1987; Schliecker et al., 1991);

◆ have greater social competency (Kontos & Fiene, 1986; Phillips et al., 1987; Vandell & Powers, 1983; White et al., 1988);

◆ have higher developmental levels of play (Melhuish et al., 1990a, 1990b; Vandell & Powers, 1983);

◆ have better ability to regulate their own behavior (Howes & Olenick, 1986; Phillips et al., 1987); and

◆ are more likely to do what they are told to do by adults (Howes & Olenick, 1986; Peterson & Peterson, 1986).

More specific information about the above studies is provided in Table 2.1, on the following page.

Table 2.1

Concurrent Research on Quality from a Global Perspective

Study	Sample	Global measure used	Findings related to children in high quality programs
Goelman & Pence, 1988	105 children of varying ages in 52 home-based settings	FDCRS	children obtained higher scores on two standard tests of language development
Howes & Olenick, 1986	57 two- and three-year-olds in 8 programs	combination of ratio, staff training, and stability	children more obedient and better able to regulate their own behavior
Kontos & Fiene, 1986, 1987	100 three-, four-, and five-year-olds, mean age of 4.4 years, in 10 programs	ECERS and a standard observational tool to rate adult behavior with children	children received higher scores on a standard measure of social skills but no difference in children's scores on tests to measure language or cognitive skills
Melhuish et al., 1990a, 1990b	34 toddlers in centers, 59 in home-based child care	combination of ratio, staff training, and the general physical space	children received higher scores on a standard measure of language development and had higher developmental levels of play
Peterson & Peterson, 1986	42 three- to five-year-olds, mean age of 4.1 years, 4 centers	combination of availability of different activities and percentage of time adults actively involved with the children	children showed higher verbal skills and were more obedient with adult requests
Phillips et al., 1987	166 children age 26 to 68 months in 9 programs	ECERS	children received higher scores on a standard measure of language development, were rated as having better social skills, and were more able to regulate their own behavior
Schliecker et al., 1991	100 four-year-olds in 10 programs	ECERS	children obtained higher scores on a standard measure of vocabulary comprehension
Vandell & Powers, 1983	53 three- and four-year-olds in 6 programs	combination of ratio, staff education, and availability of toys and equipment	children showed larger amounts of positive behavior with and towards adults, fewer incidents of negative behavior with peers, and higher developmental levels of play
White et al., 1988	60 four-year-olds in 8 programs	ECERS	children engaged in a larger proportion of positive interactions with peers

The Kontos and Fiene (1986) study, and a study by Goelman & Pence (1987), found no significant differences in children's scores on a test to measure language development between children from centers rated as high or low quality on the ECERS. In both cases, there was little variation in the total ECERS scores obtained by the "high quality" and "low quality" centers. This lack of variation may explain why there was not a statistically significant relationship between center quality and children's language scores. The above Kontos & Fiene study did find significant differences in the levels of children's social skills between centers when they used a scale that classified centers on the basis of the adult's behaviors with the children. This scale examined a number of factors believed to be associated with child development that are not rated by the ECERS.

Longitudinal Research

Longitudinal studies using a global perspective on quality in early childhood programs have demonstrated the positive impact on children of having been in a program that was classified high quality in:

◆   Canada (Jacobs et al., 1992; White, 1989);

◆   the United States (Howes, 1988; Howes, 1990; Vandell et al., 1988); and

◆   Sweden (Andersson, 1989, 1992; Broberg et al., 1989a, 1989b; Lamb et al., 1988).

The Swedish studies actually compared children who had experience in an early childhood program with children without such experience. They are being used as examples of the impact of high quality because early childhood programs in Sweden are considered by most international experts to be especially high in their quality. For example, Kammerman (1989) notes that "child care services in Sweden offer the highest quality of out-of-home care available anywhere" (page 102).

Swedish regulations require that half the staff in each group of children in center-based early childhood programs have two-and-a-half years of specialized education in child development. The remaining staff must have two years of specialized training. There can be no more than 12 children in groups where the children are under age three and there must be a staff-to-child ratio of one-to-three. The group size for children age three through six is limited to 12 (Swedish children begin formal schooling at age seven) and a ratio of one-to-four or -five (Andersson, 1989; Broberg & Hwang, 1991). Home-based child care is regulated by municipalities, many of which require the providers to take between 50 to 100 hours of specialized training. They all provide regular on-site supervision by child care experts (Andersson, 1989).

The longitudinal studies as a group demonstrate that children who were in high quality early childhood programs, when compared to peers without this experience:

◆ have greater social competency (Andersson, 1989, 1992; Howes, 1990; Lamb et al., 1988; Vandell et al., 1988; White, 1989);

◆ have fewer behavior problems in elementary school (Howes, 1988; Howes, 1990);

◆ have higher levels of language development (Jacobs et al., 1992; Andersson, 1989, 1992); and

◆ perform better in all school subjects (Andersson, 1989, 1992).

It should be noted that the Andersson study (1989, 1992) tracked children from their first year of life and reported on their progress at both age eight and age thirteen. The Swedish studies involved both home-based and center-based child care while the other studies involved only center-based programs.

More specific information about the above studies is provided in Table 2.2, on the following page.

Table 2.2

Longitudinal Research on Quality from a Global Perspective		
Study	**Sample**	**Findings related to children who had been in high quality early childhood programs**
Andersson, 1989, 1992	89 children enrolled in child care before age one, follow-up was at age eight and age thirteen	teachers rated the children as performing better in all school subjects, as more creative and socially confident, and as having better verbal skills
Broberg et al., 1989a, 1989b; Lamb et al., 1988	86 children first assessed at average age 16 months, then at 3, 12, and 24 months later	at average age of 40 months (final assessment), the children showed better social skills with peers, were rated as more mature, and had better verbal skills
Howes, 1988	75 children followed up at the end of grade one	children were rated by their teachers as having better academic skills and fewer behavior problems
Howes, 1990	80 children, 45 of whom had entered child care before age one, the others at varying ages: follow-up was at the end of kindergarten	children were rated on the basis of observation as well as teachers' questionnaires as having fewer behavior problems and better ability to focus on a task
Jacobs et al., 1992	27 children, follow-up was at the end of grade one	children received higher scores on a standard test of language development and were rated by teachers as more independent
Vandell et al., 1988	20 children who were first assessed at age three or four, follow-up was at age eight	children spent more time in positive peer interaction and were rated as having greater social competence
White, 1989	52 children, follow-up was in kindergarten	children showed a larger proportion of positive social interaction with peers and fewer incidents of negative behavior

Quality from a Non-Global Perspective

The body of research that examines quality from a global point of view is important because it demonstrates that quality in early childhood programs has similar effects on children:

- from different socioeconomic backgrounds;

- from different countries; and

- in center- or home-based child care programs.

However, this research does not tell us what *specific* aspects of the adult's behavior or the program's characteristics make a difference. Therefore, it is of limited usefulness in guiding practice or in policy development.

Chapters 3 through 6 examine the adult behaviors and specific program characteristics that have been found to have a statistically significant relationship with child well-being and development. Such studies, which look at discrete indicators of quality, generally focus on:

- the **children's daily experience**, for example, the amount and type of interaction between the adult and child or the extent to which stimulating activities are provided for the children; or

- specific **structural features** of the environment which can be clearly observed, measured, and regulated. Examples include the number of children per adult, known as the staff-to-child ratio, staff training, and the number of children in the classroom.

Children's daily experience seems to be the key to their well-being and development. The structural features of the program establish an environment that either encourages or discourages the type of daily experience that is beneficial for children. More recently, researchers have begun to examine the adult work environment and have found that aspects of it influence both adult behavior and the extent to which adults remain working in the program. Staff turnover has been shown to directly impact on child well-being and development. Chapter 7 discusses the research that has examined the impact of the adult working environment.

3 Positive Adult-Child Interaction

The relationships and interactions with the other children and the adults are the most important aspects of the child's daily experience in an early childhood program. It is these, not the toys and equipment or the building or the playground, that make up the substance of the child's experience. While relationships with other children are clearly important, the relationship with the adult may be more crucial for the young child. Much of the infant's and toddler's contact with the social and inanimate world relies on the adult's physical and/or social assistance. For children between age three and five, it is the adult who provides, or fails to provide, the sense of security necessary for the child to engage in exploration and risk-taking. These, in turn, are essential for the active involvement with the environment that is so important for learning.

Research from a Global Perspective

Research studies that use a global perspective focus on the impact of a number of different aspects of the early childhood program at the same time. For example, a researcher might study the impact on children's skill development of both the percentage of staff with college education and the number of children per staff member.

As discussed in the previous chapter, studies using a global perspective have confirmed the importance of the interaction between the adult and the child as a predictor of the child's development in:

◆ Bermuda (McCartney, 1984);

◆ Canada (Goelman & Pence, 1987);

◆ England (Melhuish, 1990a: 1990b);

◆ Israel (Rosenthal, 1991);

◆ the United States (Anderson et al., 1981; Carew, 1980; Clarke-Stewart, 1987; Golden et al., 1979; Holloway & Reichhart-Erikson, 1988; Howes, 1990; Howes & Rubenstein, 1983; Kontos, 1990; Phillips et al., 1987; Rubenstein & Howes, 1979; Ruopp et al., 1979; Tzelepis et al., 1983); and

◆ Sweden (Lamb et al., 1988).

The specific aspects of the adult's behavior that appear to have a positive impact on child well-being and development are discussed later in this chapter. Those adult behaviors that appear to have a negative impact are discussed in Chapter 4.

Some studies that have examined adult behavior with children from a global perspective on quality have found that:

◆ adult behaviors that have a positive effect on the child may be sufficiently powerful to do so regardless of whether the early childhood program has a high or low overall rating on quality and regardless of program characteristics, for example, the number of children per adult (Anderson et al., 1981; Howes, 1990); and

◆ the amount and type of interaction between the adult and preschool child can be more predictive of the child's social skills in elementary school than the type of preschool setting experienced by the child, that is: own home only, center-based child care, or home-based child care (Lamb et al., 1988).

Discrete Adult Behaviors

The research on quality from a global perspective clearly shows that the interaction between adult and child is important. However, in order to act upon this information, it is necessary to know what types of behavior make a difference. This section discusses:

◆ responsiveness;

◆ positive adult interaction;

◆ the amount and type of verbal exchange between the adult and child; and

◆ developmentally appropriate practice.

In each case, the term is defined and described before the research findings are presented.

Responsiveness

Definition and description

Responsive adults:

◆ react appropriately and promptly to children's verbal and non-verbal signals. For example, when playing peek-a-boo with an infant who then turns away, the responsive adult stops in recognition that the baby no longer wants to play that game. With an older child, the responsive adult responds to a child's request or question promptly;

◆ listen to children with attention and respect;

◆ initiate activities that are geared to the child's developmental level and interests; and

◆ are sensitive to the child's current mood and situation.

The concept of responsiveness combines three factors:

◆ age-appropriateness;

◆ appropriateness for this particular child at this time; and

◆ appropriateness in this particular situation.

Each factor is discussed separately below.

The rapidity and type of responsiveness may appropriately vary with the *child's age*. For example, an infant in distress should be picked up and comforted as quickly as possible and the source of distress attended to. Infants need to experience a consistently responsive environment in order to develop a sense of security and trust (Erikson, 1963). A gentle pat and verbal acknowledgment of the child's presence may be sufficient for a toddler who wanders over to the adult for reassurance while the adult is engaged in another task. Responsiveness with a child in kindergarten may include a short waiting period, for example, the teacher may tell the child that he or she will come over and help after getting something for another child. By age four or five, the child can wait for a few minutes as long as he or she has been assured that the request has been heard and, on the basis of past experience, is confident that it will be addressed.

An example of the issue of *a particular child at a particular time* can be illustrated by thinking of the different ways in which a toddler or preschooler may react to the loss of a staff member to whom the child has become attached. Some children may express their distress through aggression directed at other children, some children may become withdrawn and show less interest in toys and other people, others may cling to an adult. The responsive adult recognizes that, given the child's situation, the behavior being shown may be a signal that the child is in distress and in need for comfort and some extra adult support.

In a *situation* of imminent danger to a young child, responsiveness would be the immediate physical removal of the child or the source of danger. Appropriate responsiveness to a situation of two very young children fighting over a toy would be to redirect one child's attention to something else. With older children, the appropriate response in the same situation would be to help the children to verbally negotiate a solution.

Research findings

Center-based programs

In both the United States and England, a statistically significant relationship, that is, one that could not have happened by chance, has been found between responsive adults and:

◆ children who exhibit positive social skills with peers (Rubenstein & Howes, 1979; Rubenstein & Howes, 1983; Tzelepis et al., 1983; Whitebook et al., 1990); and

◆ children with higher levels of cognitive and/or language development than peers whose caregivers are less responsive (Carew, 1980; Melhuish et al., 1990a, 1990b; Rubenstein & Howes, 1983; Whitebook et al., 1990).

Infants in the Netherlands (Goosens & van IJzendoorn, 1990) and children age 10 to 56 months in the United States (Howes & Hamilton, 1992) with responsive caregivers or teachers were found to have a more secure attachment to the adult than did children whose caregivers or teachers were less responsive. A **secure attachment** is the type of relationship in which the child feels able to rely on the emotional and physical availability of the adult to provide assistance if required. Children with a secure attachment to the adult responsible for them are more likely to engage in exploration than children who lack a secure attachment to the adult (Anderson et al., 1981). Exploration of the environment is believed to assist cognitive development.

American research has found that toddlers and preschoolers with non-responsive caregivers show higher rates of **aimless wandering**, that is, unfocused behavior, than children whose caregivers are responsive (Rubenstein & Howes, 1979; Whitebook et al., 1990). Aimless wandering, in contrast to focused activity, is considered to be undesirable because it has been found to be associated with poor language development (Ruopp et al., 1979). Children with non-responsive caregivers also engage in a larger proportion of negative behaviors towards other children (Howes et al., 1988).

Home-based child care programs

A similar picture emerges in studies conducted in home-based child care. Responsive caregivers have been found to be associated with children who have:

◆ higher levels of social competence (Clarke-Stewart, 1987; Galinsky et al., 1994; Rubenstein & Howes, 1979);

◆ higher levels of intellectual skills (Clarke-Stewart, 1987; Galinsky et al., 1994); and

◆ lower levels of aimless wandering (Rubenstein & Howes, 1979).

The study by Galinsky et al. (1994) included a statistical analysis that showed that caregiver responsiveness is equally positively related to children's development whether the children are White, Black, or Latino.

Positive adult interaction

Definition and description

Positive adult interaction occurs when the adult shows active interest in the child's activities, is actively involved with the child, and provides the child with plenty of encouragement. This includes behaviors such as reading to the child, discussing with the child what the child is doing, and praising the child's efforts in trying to master a task. An example of positive adult interaction follows:

> *Jessica was new to the early childhood program and was at first hesitant to use the paints and large piece of paper that had been provided for her. With encouragement from the staff member Ann, who stayed beside her, Jessica started painting with the yellow, then stopped. Seeing there was only one brush, she dipped it into the blue paint and started to paint beside the yellow paint. Accidently, part of the blue went on top of the yellow. Jessica was clearly surprised but delighted to see the yellow become green. Ann grinned at Jessica and enthusiastically commented, " Hey —- what a terrific green you made! How did that happen?"*

Research findings

Center-based programs

When toddlers and preschoolers who experience high levels of positive adult interaction are compared with children experiencing lower levels of this adult behavior, the children show:

◆ higher rates of exploratory behavior (Anderson et al., 1981). This is considered desirable because children learn through exploration;

◆ higher levels of language development (Carew, 1980; Golden et al., 1979; Howes, 1990; Ruopp et al., 1979; Whitebook et al., 1990); and

◆ more advanced cognitive development (Carew, 1980).

Holloway & Reichhart-Erikson (1988) found a trend that almost reached the level of statistical significance between positive adult interaction and children's pro-social, rather than anti-social, responses to a test of social problem solving.

In *elementary* school, children who had experienced high rates of positive adult interaction while in child care have been rated as:

◆ having higher verbal intelligence, better ability to remain focused on a task, and more consideration for others than children whose caregivers were less involved with them (Howes, 1990); and

◆ having better social skills than children whose caregivers were less involved with them (Lamb et al., 1988).

Home-based child care programs

Clarke-Stewart (1987) found that the children who obtained the highest scores on measures of intellectual and social competence had caregivers who had more one-to-one conversations with them, touched them more, and read to them more often than did the caregivers of children with lower scores. Kontos (1990), found a statistically significant relationship between a high level of caregiver positive interaction and the children's language skills. However, the same study found that the developmental level of the children's play was lower in homes where there was a high level of positive adult interaction. In Israel, Rosenthal (1991) found that children from homes that had a high level of positive interaction between the caregiver and children were more socially competent and engaged in less aimless wandering.

Two of the above studies found a significant relationship between positive adult interaction and child social skill level (Clarke-Stewart, 1987; Rosenthal, 1991) and one found the opposite (Kontos, 1990). These conflicting findings may reflect:

♦ the use of different measures of social skills. Kontos focused on the developmental level of children's play with other children. Clarke-Stewart used a more global measure. This included the child's willingness to socialize with a strange adult, the child's ability to explain correct behavior in various social situations, and the child's social skills with peers. Similarly, Rosenthal also measured social skill level using a global measure; or

♦ the different impact of different amounts of positive adult interaction on children's peer social skills development. In her study, Clarke-Stewart noted that children in a situation of one child and one adult had poorer peer social skills than children in a setting where there were other children. Rothstein-Fisch & Howes (1988) found that children in home-based child care engaged in more complex levels of peer play when the caregiver was not actively interacting with them. These findings suggest that too much interaction between the adult and child interferes with interaction among children and may be detrimental to peer social skill building.

The amount and type of verbal exchange

Definition and description

The term **verbal exchange** implies a two-way communication between the adult and the child. Examples include the child asking a question and the adult responding, the child and adult discussing an activity they are both engaged in, or an adult engaging a child in a discussion of a picture in a book while reading a story to the child. An adult simply telling a child to do something, for example, to put on a coat, is not engaged in verbal exchange.

Studies have found a relationship between verbal exchange between the adult and child and the child's level of language and social skills. Research indicates that the key to encouraging language development is the combination of joint adult and child focus on an activity or object and the exchange of information (Carew, 1980; McCartney, 1984).

In a discussion of the development of children's peer social skills, Howes (1987) suggests that the adult acts as **an intermediary** for much of the young child's contact with the world. By this she means that the adult's physical and/or social assistance helps children in their interactions with their environment and the people in it. Social games and verbal discussions with the adult can help the child to enjoy social exchange with others. This, in turn, may encourage the child to interact with others and, in so doing, develop social competence.

Research findings

Center-based and school-based programs

The sheer amount of verbal stimulation and opportunities for two-way communication provided by the adult has been found to have a statistically significant relationship with:

◆ the child's level of language development (Carew, 1980; Golden et al., 1979; McCartney, 1984; Melhuish et al., 1990a, 1990b; Rubenstein & Howes, 1983; Ruopp et al., 1979); and

◆ the child's level of social competence (Clarke-Stewart, 1987; Golden et al., 1979; Phillips et al., 1987).

Home-based child care

Clarke-Stewart (1987) found that the children in home-based settings who scored the highest on assessments of intellectual and social competence had caregivers who had more one-to-one conversations with the children than did the other caregivers in her sample.

Developmentally appropriate practice

Definition and description

The United States' Association for the Education of Young Children and the Association for Childhood Education International both advocate the use of developmentally appropriate practice in early childhood programs. Position papers from each organization state that quality experiences for kindergarten and pre-kindergarten children must be based upon expectations and practices that are consistent with what is known about how children develop and learn (Bredekamp, 1987; Moyer et al., 1987).

However, although research has demonstrated predictable stages that occur in children's development in the physical, emotional, social, language, and cognitive areas, individual children proceed at different rates. For example, by approximately the middle of the first year, babies put together consonant-vowel combinations, such as "ma-ma-ma", which sound speech-like and are referred to as "babbling". Somewhere between 12 and 18 months, most children say their first clearly recognizable words, usually the names of familiar persons or things. This "labeling" ability is followed by combining two words together in a way that conveys meaning, for example, the toddler who insists "me do". Between age two and three-and-a-half, children's vocabularies grow rapidly, as do their abilities to construct longer and more grammatically correct sentences. While the above is the predictable sequence in language development for all children, the age at which an individual child begins labeling or combining words together varies.

There are also predictable stages in the physical, emotional, social, and cognitive areas. Again, individual children vary in the age at which they reach certain stages. Children also may vary in their skill levels across developmental areas. For example, a child may have language skills that are advanced for his or her age but lag behind age-mates in social skills. As a result, developmentally appropriate practice must consider what is appropriate for an individual child as well as what is known about universal patterns of development.

Developmentally appropriate practice can be defined as an approach to working with young children that requires the adult to pay attention to both:

◆ what is appropriate to expect *from* and *to do* with a child of a given age; and

◆ what is appropriate for an individual child based on knowledge of that child's abilities, needs, background, and interests.

The concept of developmental appropriateness owes much to the research and theory of Jean Piaget (1950, 1972) who concluded that:

◆ children learn through concrete exploration and manipulation of their environments;

◆ children have an inborn natural motivation to strive to understand their surroundings and to make sense of what they observe and experience; and

◆ children's ability to understand depends upon their maturational level; therefore, certain cognitive skills must be present before a child can understand certain concepts.

An important aspect of developmentally appropriate practice is the belief that children's skill development is encouraged by providing:

◆ an environment rich in a variety of things to explore; and

◆ an atmosphere that encourages and supports the child to exercise his or her curiosity.

Unfortunately, this belief is sometimes over-simplified to the point of being interpreted to mean that encouraging child-initiated learning through exploration and manipulation means prohibiting teacher-directed activity. Bredekamp (1991, 1993) points out that, in fact, adult input is crucial. However, it must be provided in ways suited to the child's level of learning and development. For kindergarten and pre-kindergarten age children, this means setting up a variety of opportunities for exploration and problem solving, asking open-ended questions, and offering suggestions. Heavy reliance on strategies such as drill in recognizing letters is not developmentally appropriate for children of this age.

Research findings

All the research regarding developmentally appropriate practice has been conducted in child care centers or kindergarten programs. Whitebook et al. (1990), in a study that involved 227 child care centers in five different cities in the United States, found a statistically significant relationship between high levels of developmentally appropriate practice and high levels of appropriate peer play and language development. The same association was found for infants, toddlers, and preschoolers. Love (1993) found that four-year-olds in classrooms where the activities were not developmentally appropriate showed higher rates of stress behaviors than peers in other classes. Haskins (1985) compared children from a variety of child care centers when they were in elementary school. He found that those who had attended child care programs that stressed cognitive development and involved an emphasis on academic skill building showed higher rates of aggression than children whose child care experience had been more age-appropriate.

In an assessment of 204 kindergarten children, Burts et al. (1992) found that children in classrooms where the programming was not developmentally appropriate showed higher levels of stress than did children in classes that were developmentally appropriate. In a second study involving 103 kindergarten classrooms, Bryant et al. (1991) found that the teacher's knowledge of developmentally appropriate practice was a better predictor of classroom score on a global measure of quality than was the teacher's level of education, years of experience teaching kindergarten, or years of teaching experience in general.

What Predicts Positive Adult Behaviors?

Research studies have found a statistically significant relationship between positive adult behaviors and:

◆ education in child development and/or early childhood programming; and

◆ the number of children with whom the adult is in contact.

Education

Adults who have training in child development and/or early childhood programing have been found more likely to exhibit positive adult behaviors with and towards children than child care staff or kindergarten teachers without such training. This relationship has been found in Canada, Bermuda, and the United States. It holds true for center-based, school-based, and home-based early childhood programs and in regard to children from infancy through age five (Arnett, 1989; Berk, 1985; Fosburg, 1981; Galinsky et al., 1994; Howes, 1983; Jones & Meisels, 1987; Pence & Goelman, 1991; Ruopp et al., 1979; Stuart & Pepper, 1988; Whitebook et al., 1990). The finding that education related to child development is important is not surprising. Such education assists the adult in understanding children's developmental stages. Therefore, the education increases the likelihood that the adult will be able to accurately interpret the child's behavior, will not impose unrealistic expectations, and will engage in developmentally appropriate practice.

The number of children

The definition of what is a reasonable number of children for one adult to be responsible for (the staff-to-child ratio) varies with the children's ages. The differences in appropriate staff-to-child ratios for different ages are discussed in Chapter 6. Research from Canada, the United States, and England has found that a reasonable staff-to-child ratio is associated with adults who:

◆ are responsive (Howes, 1983; Howes & Rubenstein, 1985; Kontos & Fiene, 1987; Whitebook et al., 1990); and

◆ are actively involved with the children (Biemiller et al., 1976; Howes, 1983; Ruopp et al., 1979; Sylva et al., 1980).

The definition of what is a reasonable number of children in a group or classroom also depends on the child's age and is also discussed in Chapter 6. Research in the United States found that:

- in groups of 12 or fewer three- to five-year-olds, the adults were more actively involved with the children than were the adults with groups of 24 of more children (Ruopp et al., 1979). In this study, the benefit of smaller group (classroom) size was observed even when the staff-to-child ratio was held constant. In other words, the adult behaviors were more positive in situations of one adult with eight children than in situations of three adults for twenty-four children, even though the ratio was 1:8 in each situation; and

- there is a significant relationship between a reasonable group or classroom size and adult responsiveness (Howes, 1983; Kontos & Fiene, 1987).

A small group, or responsibility for only a small number of children, provides a greater opportunity for the adult to be involved with the children and their activities and to have real conversations with them. Research has shown that adults responsible for large groups of children spend a higher percentage of their time simply controlling the children, and a smaller percentage of their time in social stimulation or program activities, than do adults working with smaller groups of children (Biemiller et al., 1976; Field, 1980; Melhuish et al., 1990b; Ruopp et al., 1979; Sylva et al., 1980).

Implications for Practice

Responsiveness, positive adult interaction, true verbal exchange, and developmentally appropriate practice all assist the child's well-being and development. Therefore, they are all behaviors we should try to use when working with children. Responsiveness and positive adult interaction may be beneficial because they give the child the feeling of being cared *about* as well as cared for. This, in turn, could be expected to increase self-confidence and self-esteem and to encourage exploratory behavior. Verbal exchange and developmentally appropriate practice help the child to build on existing skills. They also provide the child with a model of competent behavior. For example, the adult provides the child with a model of sentence construction as he or she talks with the child.

Research studies clearly demonstrate a relationship between education in child development or early childhood programming and the likelihood of positive adult behaviors. This relationship has been found both in regard to basic training before starting a career and to on-going professional development after basic training through workshops and seminars. While it has not been explicitly demonstrated, it is probable that an important factor is training related to the age of the children being served. Given the great changes that occur in children during early childhood, it is unreasonable to expect that someone trained to work with infants and toddlers is equally knowledgeable about five-year-olds. Similarly, someone used to seven- and eight-year-olds may have difficulty knowing what is developmentally appropriate practice with four-year-olds.

4 Negative Adult–Child Interaction

As noted in the previous chapter, the relationships and interactions with the other children and adults are the most important aspects of the child's daily experience in an early childhood program. This holds true whether the program is home-based, school-based, or in a child care center. For young children, the type of interaction with the adult is crucial in assisting or impeding the child's basic well-being and development.

◆ ◆ ◆ ◆ Discrete Types of Negative Adult Behavior

Research has demonstrated three discrete adult behaviors that have a negative impact on children enrolled in early childhood programs, namely:

- ◆ detachment;
- ◆ restrictiveness; and
- ◆ harshness.

This chapter discusses these three behaviors. Each behavior is defined and described before the research findings are presented.

Detachment

Definition and description

Adult detachment is the opposite of the positive adult interaction described in the previous chapter. **Detachment** refers to an observable lack of involvement by the adult with the child. It may be lack of verbal and/or emotional involvement, even while being physically involved, or lack of any interaction. Two examples of detachment versus positive adult interaction follow. In the first example, note the contrast between the detachment shown by Mrs. Smith and Mrs. Lee and the active interest and involvement of Mrs. Xenakis. Peter, in the second example, shows both positive involvement and responsiveness. In contrast, Gina is physically involved with Halina but not emotionally or verbally engaged with her.

Mrs. Xenakis, Mrs. Smith, and Mrs. Lee are supervising the junior kindergarten children during recess in the school yard. Mrs. Smith and Mrs. Lee are off to one side talking animatedly with each other. As a result, they are not paying full attention to what the children are doing. Mrs. Xenakis is helping a group of children build a snow fort. She had joined in their discussion of where to locate the fort. Now she is helping them to make snow blocks and put them in place. At the same time, she is verbally encouraging the children in their efforts.

Gina and Peter are in the changing room of the child care center at the same time. While Gina changes Halina's diaper, Peter is changing Tony. Gina works quickly and without a word to Halina or even much eye contact. Initially, Halina watches Gina and babbles. However, getting no response to her efforts to socialize, Halina turns her head away to watch Peter and Tony. As Peter is changing Tony, he talks softly to him. When Tony grabs a piece of the clean diaper and puts it over his face, Peter joins in the game by saying, "Where's Tony? Tony has gone!" Peter then gently pulls the diaper away and remarks, "There's Tony." Tony responds by laughing.

Research findings

All the research to date on the impact of adult detachment has been conducted in center-based child care settings. A statistically significant relationship has been found between adult detachment and toddlers and preschoolers who show:

- poor language development (Ruopp et al., 1979; Whitebook et al., 1990);

- lower developmental levels of play (Whitebook et al., 1990);

- higher rates of disobedience than their peers (Peterson & Peterson, 1986); and

- high rates of aimless wandering rather than focused activity (Ruopp et al., 1979; Whitebook et al., 1990).

A child who is engaged in aimless wandering is not interacting with either people or things in a focused way. As a result, the child is not taking advantage of any opportunities the environment may provide for skill development.

Restrictiveness

Definition and description

Restrictiveness can involve either:

- what the adult allows or does not allow the child to do; and/or

- what materials and opportunities are or are not provided for the child.

Restrictive behavior is controlling and includes: telling a child not to touch something, or not to do something, or removing something from a child. Sometimes there are valid safety reasons associated with an adult's restrictiveness. However, restrictiveness is classified as a negative adult behavior when it is frequent or occurs when there is no safety issue involved. A restrictive adult would react to a two-year-old wanting to explore a climbing apparatus by saying "no". A non-restrictive adult would help the child to do what was within his or her capabilities and would address the potential safety issue by remaining close to the child to provide assistance if needed.

Restrictiveness can also involve deliberately limiting children's opportunities for exploration. For example, the adult who provides blocks, paper, and crayons for the children, but will not provide paints or a sand box because they are "too messy" is being restrictive.

Research findings

Research on the impact of restrictiveness has only been done in child care settings and has involved primarily toddlers and preschoolers. The exception is a study conducted in Bermuda that involved children ranging in age from 36 to 68 months (McCartney, 1984). Adult restrictiveness has been found to be associated with children who have:

◆ poor language development (Berk, 1985; Carew, 1980; McCartney, 1984);

◆ poorer performance on tests of cognitive skills than children whose caregivers were not restrictive (Clarke-Stewart, 1987); and

◆ behavior problems at a later age (Rubenstein & Howes, 1983).

Clarke-Stewart's study involved both home-based and center-based child care, and her findings pertain to both types of settings.

Harshness

Harsh adults are critical with the children, scold or threaten them, and/or use punishment as a means of discipline. **Harshness** can be conveyed by tone of voice as well as by words or action.

In the United States, a significant relationship has been found between harsh adults and preschoolers who show higher levels of aimless wandering than do children whose caregivers are not harsh. The children were also found to be less attached to their caregiver (Whitebook et al., 1990). Both aimless wandering and lack of attachment to the caregiver are believed to have a negative impact on child well-being and development. A second American study found that four-year-olds in classrooms with harsh teachers showed more evidence of stress behaviors than did peers in classes where the adult was not harsh (Love, 1993).

What Predicts Negative Adult Behaviors?

Research studies have found a statistically significant relationship between negative adult behaviors and:

◆ lack of education in child development or early childhood programing; and

◆ certain aspects of the environment, namely: responsibility for too many children, too many children in one class or setting even though the adult-to-child ratio is appropriate, or a setting that is unsafe for children.

Education

Adults without education in child development or early childhood programing have been found to be more likely to show adult behaviors that impede child well-being and development than adults with such education. This relationship has been found in Canada, Bermuda, and the United States and holds true for center-based, school-based, and home-based early childhood programs and in regard to children from infancy through age five (Arnett, 1987; Berk, 1985; Fosburg, 1981; Howes, 1983; Jones & Meisels, 1987; Pence & Goelman, 1991; Ruopp et al., 1979; Stuart & Pepper, 1988; Whitebook et al., 1990).

Education may make a difference for a variety of reasons, for example, because:

◆ it helps the person to be realistic in his or her expectations of what the child can do, thereby lessening the likelihood of the adult becoming restrictive, harsh, or frustrated with the child;

◆ it provides the adult with information about positive strategies for encouraging desired child behavior; and

◆ it impresses upon the adult the fact that the adult's physical presence is not sufficient, in itself, to foster child well-being and development.

Certain aspects of the environment

Responsibility for too many children

The definition of what is a reasonable number of children for one adult to be responsible for depends on the children's ages. The differences in appropriate staff-to-child ratios for different ages is discussed in Chapter 6. Research from Canada, the United States, and England has found that too many children per adult is related to:

◆ adults who are harsh (Whitebook et al., 1990) or restrictive (Howes & Rubenstein, 1985; Smith & Connolly, 1986);

◆ adults who are detached (Howes et al., 1988; Whitebook et al., 1990); and

◆ a higher percentage of the adult's time being spent in restricting and controlling the children, and less time spent in providing social or other stimulation (Biemiller et al., 1976; Field, 1980; Melhuish et al., 1990b; Ruopp et al., 1979; Smith & Connolly, 1986; Sylva et al., 1980).

Too many children in one class or setting

The definition of too many children in a group or class also depends on age. Appropriate class sizes are discussed in Chapter 6. Research from the United States has found a relationship between a large number of children in a group or classroom and adults who are:

◆ restrictive (Howes, 1983; Howes & Rubenstein, 1985); or

◆ detached (Howes, 1983; Howes, & Rubenstein, 1985; Kontos & Fiene, 1987).

Ruopp et al. (1979) found that, in groups of 24 or more three- to five-year-olds, the adults spent a higher percentage of their time in control-ling and monitoring the children than did adults with groups of 12 or fewer children. It is noteworthy that the impact of the larger groups was observed even when the staff-to-child ratio was the same. In other words, the adult behaviors were more positive in situations of one adult with 8 children than in situations of three adults for 24 children, even though the staff-to-child ratio was 1:8 in each situation.

Setting size also makes a difference. Prescott et al. (1967), in a report summarizing data from 50 child care centers in the United States, found that centers with over 60 children:

◆ had staff members who were more often rated as detached and were twice as restrictive and controlling than staff in smaller centers; and

◆ placed greater emphasis on routines and group activities versus individual activities than did centers with 30 to 60 children.

More recently, both Moore (1987) and Kontos & Fiene (1987) found that staff in large centers tended to be more restrictive and controlling than those in smaller centers.

An unsafe environment

Home-based child care providers working in child-designated space that is safe for children have been found to be less likely to restrict chil-dren's activities than child care providers working in an unsafe setting (Howes, 1983).

Observations

Responsibility for too many children or an unsafe environment:

◆ puts the adult in a situation where it is difficult to ensure the child's safety. The likelihood of restrictiveness is increased when it is easi-er to forbid an action than to provide the supervision that enables the child to safely engage in the activity; and

◆ puts stress on the adult which may, in turn, increase the possibility of harshness.

Too many children in one setting may have a negative impact on adult behavior regardless of the staff-to-child ratio because, past a certain size, the number of children relative to their need for supervision and assistance becomes overwhelming for the adults. Some adults may respond to the implicit demands of such a situation by detachment.

♦ ♦ ♦ ♦ Implications for Practice

Adult detachment, restrictiveness, and harshness all impede the child's well-being and development. Detachment may impede child well-being and development in one of two ways. First of all, it may give the child the implicit message that the adult does not really care about him or her. Secondly, it results in the possibility that the adult will not be available when needed, for example, when the child is being verbally bullied by another child. Experiences such as this make it difficult for the child to feel confident about the adult's availability.

Restrictiveness and harshness may have a negative effect on children because they discourage the exploration believed by Piaget (1950, 1972) to be very important for cognitive development. The child who is constantly told not to touch something, especially if the request is accompanied by a warning that "you might hurt yourself", gradually stops reaching out to explore. Similarly, the child whose exploratory behaviors result in scolding or criticism is likely to decide that exploration is a bad thing to do because it makes adults angry.

A statistically significant relationship has been found between adult behaviors, both those that encourage and those that impede child well-being and development, and whether staff have education in child development and early childhood programing. Adult behavior is also influenced by: the staff-to-child ratio, the number of children in one class or setting, and the safety of the environment. The type of interaction between the adult and child in turn predicts the child's well-being and development. These relationships are illustrated in Fig. 4.1, on the following page.

Figure 4.1

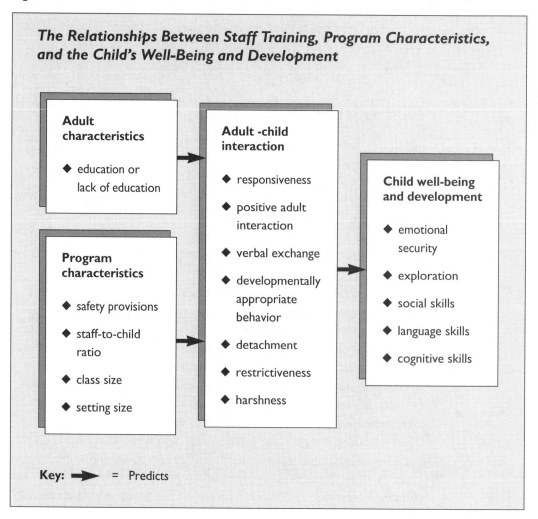

The Relationships Between Staff Training, Program Characteristics, and the Child's Well-Being and Development

Adult characteristics

◆ education or lack of education

Program characteristics

◆ safety provisions

◆ staff-to-child ratio

◆ class size

◆ setting size

Adult -child interaction

◆ responsiveness

◆ positive adult interaction

◆ verbal exchange

◆ developmentally appropriate behavior

◆ detachment

◆ restrictiveness

◆ harshness

Child well-being and development

◆ emotional security

◆ exploration

◆ social skills

◆ language skills

◆ cognitive skills

Key: ➡ = Predicts

5

Other Important Aspects of the Child's Daily Experience

Chapters 3 and 4 stressed the importance of the interaction between the adult and child in the child's daily experience. Other important aspects are:

◆ parent involvement in the early childhood program;

◆ staff consistency;

◆ programing; and

◆ the physical environment.

The following four sections discuss these four aspects. Each section presents a definition, research findings, and implications for practice. Where relevant, current theory is also discussed.

Parent Involvement

Definition

Parent involvement is a term that covers a range of activities including:

◆ parents simply receiving periodic newsletters from the program;

◆ regular meetings between the parent and the program staff to exchange information about the child;

◆ the provision of occasional assistance on field trips by the parent;

◆ the parent as a volunteer in the program on a regular basis; and

◆ parents in a decision-making capacity, for example, on a parent advisory committee or the board of directors of a child care center.

Theory

Parent involvement addresses the second part of the definition of a high quality early childhood program given in Chapter 1, that is: a program that "supports and complements the family in its child-rearing role". The theory supporting parental involvement emphasizes its value in:

◆ increasing consistency and predictability for the child; and

◆ sharing knowledge and expertise so that both the parent and the program are supported in their roles.

With higher levels of workforce participation by the mothers of young children than in the past, child rearing is increasingly a joint endeavor between parents and early childhood programs. As a result, many children have two key socializing agents. Some children have more than two because they are enrolled in child care and kindergarten or in multiple child care programs at the same time. On the basis of a number of studies conducted in the United States, Powell (1989, page 32) concludes:

the existing evidence suggests that family and early childhood programs constitute different social environments for children in terms of childrearing values, behavioral expectations, and patterns of adult-child interaction.

Cloutier (1985), in Canada, agrees that lack of continuity may exist between the home and the early childhood setting. She suggests that when the lack of continuity is moderate or severe, the effectiveness of both the home and the early childhood program is reduced. Children may become bewildered, confused, and anxious if there are major differences between what happens or is expected at home and what happens or is expected in the early childhood program. Therefore, one of the strongest arguments for meaningful on-going communication between the parent and the early childhood program is the expectation that this will increase the continuity of the child's experience. The underlying assumption is that parent and staff member share information and are able to agree on consistent approaches with the child. The likelihood of this being important is evident in basic socialization tasks, for example, toilet training and learning to take responsibility for putting on one's own coat.

Parents and staff each have their own knowledge of the child. Parents know their child's history, part of which may be very relevant to how the child adjusts to a new early childhood program, their child's personality, and what is going on in the home. Staff know about child development, have experience with children in general, and know what is happening in the early childhood program. As noted by Whitebook et al. (1989), without on-going communication, neither the parents nor the program staff have the total picture. Bredekamp (1987) suggests that it is especially important that parents and staff frankly discuss basic values and childrearing practices when infants and toddlers are concerned. She notes that during these early years, children learn whether or not their environment is supportive and predictable. Parents and staff who frequently share information about the child's routines and daily experiences increase the likelihood that the child will experience a reasonably consistent environment. With older children, knowing that a child had a fight with his best friend at the early childhood program may help the parent to understand and handle an evening upset. Similarly, it is helpful for a teacher to know when a child slept poorly because his baby brother cried all night.

Theory also supports the practice of having parents in a decision-making role, for example, as members of a parent advisory committee or as members of a child care center's board of directors. This type of parent involvement is believed to encourage quality by providing a parental view and by giving parents a voice in policy and program development (Gagné, 1989). It may be especially valuable when the early childhood program serves children from other cultures. Information from the parents can help the staff to understand culturally specific ways of communicating and cultural behavior expectations.

Research findings

Longitudinal studies of American compensatory preschool programs for children at environmental risk have found some positive effects on parental childrearing practices from involvement in the program (Berrueta-Clement et al., 1984; Love et al., 1976). However, the programs in question were demonstration projects and often involved one or more of: specific parent skill training, regular home visits, or the parent observing and helping in the classroom. Since these programs were not typical of programs generally available in their community, the research findings may not apply to ordinary community-based programs.

Smith & Hubbard (1988), in a study conducted in five ordinary community kindergartens involving 60 children in New Zealand, examined the relationship between child behavior and the following four aspects of the observed communication between parents and teachers:

◆ the sheer amount (that is, the frequency and duration of the communication);

◆ the extent to which there was a real two-way discussion of substantive issues and real involvement of parents in decision making (that is, whether the relationship was reciprocal);

◆ the extent to which feelings between teacher and parent appeared to be warm and positive rather than negative or hostile (that is, whether or not the relationship was warm); and

◆ the extent to which there was an equal relationship with neither party dominating or failing to respect the other (that is, whether the relationship was balanced).

Kindergartens with larger amounts of communication between teachers and parents had children who interacted more with their teachers. Where there was a balanced, reciprocal relationship and/or a warm relationship between parent and teacher, the incidence of positive peer interactions by the child was higher.

In an American study, Hogan (1991) examined the relationship between parents and caregivers in 25 regulated home-based child care settings that had at least one three- or four-year-old. She also took observations of the interactions between the caregiver and children in each home. The children whose parents and caregivers talked most with each other showed the highest rates of positive interaction with both the caregiver and the other children in the home. No differences were found in the caregiver's behavior with the child, frequency of conversations with the child, amount of teaching, or approach to discipline. The two above studies suggest that communication between the parent and the early childhood program staff member has a positive effect on the child's interactions with other children.

Friesen (1992), in Canada, and Howes (1986), in the United States, found that early childhood programs with a high global rating on quality provided parents with a variety of opportunities for input into decision making. The opportunities included: individual discussions with the child's primary caregiver, periodic meetings with the program's director, and representation on a parent advisory committee or the center's board of directors. These findings suggest a link between quality and parent involvement in a decision-making capacity. However, it is difficult to know if the high global rating on quality resulted from parent involvement, or if high quality programs are more likely to actively seek parent involvement in decision making.

What predicts whether program staff will promote parent involvement?

The early childhood program's staff members are the key figures in fostering parent involvement. They provide, or fail to provide, an environment where the parent feels welcomed, valued, and perceived as a partner. Swick & McKnight (1989) studied 45 certified kindergarten teachers working in different schools to determine the factors associated with teacher promotion of parent involvement. They found that:

♦ teachers who had been trained in early childhood education, whose experience had been primarily in preschool and kinder-garten settings, and who were working in an environment that encouraged parent involvement were more likely to be supportive of parent involvement and to feel that it was important to establish a partnership with the parent; and

♦ teachers who had worked primarily in the elementary grades, who had a relatively large class, and who were working in an environ-ment that did not actively support parent involvement were less likely to be supportive of parent involvement.

These findings illustrate the importance of the program's administra-tion actively encouraging and supporting parent involvement.

Implications for practice

Observational studies in the United States have found that the most frequent time for information exchange between parent and staff member in child care centers is when the child is dropped off or picked up (Galinsky, 1988). However, this is precisely the time that many cen-ters reduce adult-to-child ratios on the assumption that there are fewer children. Furthermore, parents may feel pressured by the need to get to their own work when dropping off their child and pressured by the need to get home to prepare supper when picking up the child.

In an American study involving 16 child care centers, Endsley & Minish (1991) found that the average length of conversation between caregiver and parents at drop-off or pick-up was 12 seconds. Sixty-three percent of all "conversations" were greetings or small talk, not substantive exchange of information. In 43 percent of the situations observed, the parent and caregiver did not even greet each other. This study and those cited by Galinsky (1988) suggest the need to deliber-ately plan parent involvement both at drop-off and pick-up and at other times.

Mayfield (1990) notes that there is no "right" way of implementing parent involvement. Even within a given program, there may be a need to provide for a variety of types and levels of parent involvement in order to meet individual situations. Mayfield suggests that when trying to encourage parent involvement, programs consider:

◆ the parents' wishes and the parents' availability in light of their family and work commitments; and

◆ what the program requires.

It is essential to recognize that parents need an orientation before becoming part of a parent advisory committee or board of directors. Many will need training regarding the roles and responsibilities they are assuming, especially since this is often the first time the parent has served in this type of decision-making capacity.

◆ ◆ ◆ ◆ # Staff Consistency

Definition

The term "staff consistency" is often used to mean staff turnover, that is, the frequency with which staff leave the program. However, from the child's point of view, lack of consistency also occurs if the child is moved frequently from one group or class to another or if the staff frequently rotate within a program. Finally, staffing inconsistency can be related to the frequent movement of children from one program to another by their parents.

Theory

Just as relationships between adults are based on what they do together and their interactions over time, the relationship between a child and adult is built on what is shared together and the child's experience of that adult. When the adult, whether parent or another, is consistently responsive and available when needed, the child develops what Bowlby (1969/1982) calls a secure attachment to the adult. The term "secure attachment" refers to the child's trust that the adult will be responsive and available for support. If the adult ignores or rejects the child's signals for assistance, or response is a hit-or-miss affair, or there are frequent changes among adults, the child will develop either an **anxious** or an **insecure attachment**.

As noted by Melhuish et al. (1990a), an adult who is involved with a child on a frequent basis comes to understand the child's non-verbal as well as verbal ways of communicating needs. This understanding increases the probability that the adult will be responsive. Responsiveness, in turn, fosters the development of a secure attachment. As noted below, a secure attachment appears to increase the likelihood of exploration by the child, a behavior that Piaget (1950) believed was very important for cognitive development.

Research findings

Research has clearly demonstrated that infants and toddlers in early childhood programs can and do form secure attachments with both their parents and their child care providers at the same time (Ainslie & Anderson, 1984; Anderson et al., 1981; Goosens & van IJzendoorn, 1990; Howes et al., 1988; Howes & Hamilton, 1992).

Children with a secure attachment to their caregiver behave as if they derive emotional security from the adult's presence. Anderson et al. (1981) found that children ranging in age from 19 to 42 months who had a secure attachment to their caregiver engaged in significantly larger amounts of exploratory behavior than did children lacking this type of attachment. In a second American study, Howes et al. (1988) examined the child's attachment to both the mother and to the caregiver among children ranging in age from 13 to 28 months. They found a statistically significant relationship between a secure attachment to *both* the mother and the caregiver and the amount of time the child engaged in play with peers while in the child care setting. An insecure attachment with *either* adult was associated with less peer involvement by the child. However, "the security of attachment to the caregiver was somewhat more influential in determining engagement with peers than security of attachment to mother" (page 414). No differences were found in child social behavior as a function of the type of setting (home- or center-based), the age the child entered child care, the length of time the child had spent in the setting, or the number of hours per week that the child was enrolled.

Four studies from the United States have looked at the impact of staff consistency. A statistically significant relationship was found between consistency of the primary caregiver and:

◆ more social interactions with the adult by children aged 18 to 24 months (Howes & Rubenstein, 1985);

◆ less anxiety and fewer stress behaviors, for example, crying or pulling away, by children aged 4 to 28 months when dropped off at the center by the mother (Cummings, 1980); and

◆ children exhibiting less social withdrawal and aggression at age four than peers who had experienced less staff consistency (Howes & Hamilton, 1993).

In their study of 227 child care centers, Whitebook et al. (1990) found that children in centers that had experienced a *high* staff turnover in the previous twelve months:

◆ showed less secure attachments to their caregivers;

◆ spent significantly less time engaged in social activities and more time in aimless wandering than did children in centers with lower staff turnover rates;

◆ had lower developmental levels of peer play;

◆ received lower scores on a standard measure of language development than did age-mates in other centers; and

◆ had a lower perception of their own competence.

Howes & Hamilton (1993) hypothesized that staff changes would be more disadvantageous to younger than older children because younger children, being less mobile and having less developed social skills, are more dependent on adults. They tested this hypothesis by studying children for a three-year period. They found that children who experienced a change in caregiver between age 18 and 24 months, regardless of the quality of their attachment to the caregiver, were more likely to be aggressive than children who did not experience staff turnover at this age.

What predicts staff turnover?

Research has demonstrated that high rates of staff turnover in a program are associated with:

◆ low salaries and poor benefit packages (Canadian Child Care Federation/Canadian Child Care Advocacy Association, 1992; Kontos & Stremmel, 1988; Schom-Moffat, 1984; Stremmel, 1991; Whitebook et al., 1982; Whitebook et al., 1990);

◆ poor working conditions, for example, too many children per staff member (Kontos & Stremmel, 1988; Maslach & Pines, 1977; Smith & Connolly, 1986; Whitebook et al., 1990);

◆ lack of opportunities for input into the program's policy development and program planning (Maslach & Pines, 1977; Whitebook et al., 1982; Whitebook et al., 1990); and

◆ a feeling of lack of feedback or support from the center director (Stremmel, 1991) or poor communication patterns among staff (Kontos & Stremmel, 1988).

Implications for practice

The research underlines the importance of staff consistency both between individual children and adults and within the early childhood program as a whole. Stability of the relationship between child and adult may be safeguarded by:

◆ reducing the frequency of staff rotation between groups or classrooms; and

◆ reducing the frequency with which children change groups or classrooms.

Traditionally, most early childhood programs are organized by age group. Therefore, periodic moves do happen. Howes & Hamilton (1993) suggest that the potentially disruptive impact of this practice on young children may be lessened by allowing the child to have regular visits to his or her previous teacher. Similarly, where possible, allowing a child to spend some time in his or her new group or classroom before actually moving to it may ease the transition.

Katz et al. (1990) advocate the use of mixed-aged groups in early childhood programs. These allow a child to remain with the same adult throughout the preschool period. The use of mixed-aged groups is discussed in more detail in the final chapter of this book.

Mechanisms to reduce staff turnover in a program are discussed in Chapter 7.

◆ ◆ ◆ ◆ Programming

Definition

Programming, sometimes referred to as the curriculum, includes all the various routines and activities that form part of the child's daily experience. While programming is often thought of in a formal, academic way, with young children it includes hygiene and other routines. These routines not only provide the structure that helps the child to feel secure, but they also provide opportunities for skill development. For example, if the adult talks to the child and responds to the child's babbling, diaper changing can be used to encourage language development as well as self-help skills, for example, undressing.

Theory

Bredekamp & Rosegrant (1992) observe that there can be one of two basic problems with the programming in early childhood programs, namely:

◆ inadequate attention to the content of the programming, for example, large amounts of time for child-chosen activities with little attempt to guide the activities to provide learning opportunities. This can result in a haphazard rather than a purposeful experience; or

♦ over-attention to the content of the programming and to adult-determined goals and objectives. This can result in activities that are not developmentally appropriate or fail to accommodate cultural variations in learning style.

Therefore, it is important to balance:

♦ the fact that children discover concepts spontaneously through their own initiated interaction with, and manipulation of, the environment; and

♦ children's need for adults to guide their exploration and to specifically instruct them in the many things that are necessary for survival in their society.

As noted by Bredekamp (1993), "child-initiated learning does not occur in the absence of teacher guidance or input" (page 118). In other words, it is not sufficient to provide a variety of stimulating materials and an environment that encourages exploration and interaction. The adult must select and prepare the environment, then observe, guide, and assist the children so that they are challenged and supported in gaining information and an understanding of how things work.

Research findings

Studies in the United States, England, and Bermuda have found a statistically significant relationship between a program that includes organized activities and adult-determined goals and children who obtain higher scores on tests of language and/or cognitive skills than peers in programs that involve mainly free play (Carew, 1980; Clarke-Stewart & Gruber, 1984; McCartney, 1984; Ruopp et al., 1979; Smith and Connolly, 1986).

Two American studies support the importance of balancing adult-determined goals with child-initiated activities. Haskins (1985) compared children from a variety of child care centers when they were in elementary school. He found that those who had attended programs with a high proportion of adult-initiated activities showed higher rates of aggression than did peers from other programs. In a second longitudinal study, children were randomly assigned to preschools with different types of programming (Schweinhart et al., 1986). At age 15, the adolescents who had been in highly adult-structured early childhood programs, when compared to peers who had been in programs where the children initiated and paced their own learning activities within a context provided by the adult:

◆ had been involved in twice as many delinquent acts; and

◆ had poorer relationships with their families.

Implications for practice

The research indicates that children are most likely to benefit from a predictable daily program that combines organized activities with some flexibility for children to choose what they want to do and to explore at their own pace.

The Physical Environment

Definition

The physical environment refers to both the inside and outside space, and the availability of toys and equipment.

Research findings

Studies have found that both child development and adult behavior are influenced by the organization of the early childhood program's setting and the materials available in it. The findings of this research are discussed under the following sub-headings:

◆ findings related to center-based or school-based settings;

◆ findings related to home-based child care; and

◆ findings related to the different impact on children of different types of toys and equipment.

Center-based and school-based settings

Moore (1986) studied the impact of what he called "well-defined behavior settings" versus "poorly defined behavior settings" by observing staff and children in 14 programs serving children age 18 months to 6 years. Well-defined settings had:

◆ clear boundaries and separation between circulation space, group space, and activity pockets;

◆ at least partial acoustic separation of areas for small group and for large group activities;

◆ space sizes that were appropriate for the activity for which they were intended, for example, large space for large group or high-energy level activities;

◆ an appropriate amount and type of storage, work surface, and display space;

◆ materials for use by the children located so as to be readily accessible by them, for example, on low shelves that the children could reach; and

◆ variations in floor coverings, textures, and levels, for example, a loft and/or a sunken pit area.

Moore found a statistically significant relationship between well-defined behavior settings, versus poorly defined behavior settings, and

◆ larger amounts of adult positive involvement with children as opposed to detachment or restrictive behavior;

◆ more child exploratory behavior, that is, investigating, examining, asking questions, and manipulating objects;

◆ more social interaction among the children; and

◆ a larger proportion of cooperative interaction among the children.

Three other pieces of American research specifically demonstrate improvements in child behavior when large spaces are partitioned to form smaller activity areas, namely:

◆ increased rates of cooperative interaction among the children (Field, 1980; Rohe & Nuffer, 1977);

- decreased rates of unfocused activity or simply standing and observing others (Holloway & Reichhart-Erickson, 1988; Rohe & Nuffer, 1977); and

- reduced rates of aggression among the children (Rohe & Nuffer, 1977).

Clarke-Stewart (1987) found that children demonstrated better social and cognitive skills when they were in centers that were orderly, had varied and stimulating toys and materials, and in which the space was organized into activity areas.

Home-based child care

Clarke-Stewart & Gruber (1984) examined the impact of the physical environment on two- and three-year-olds using the following five measures: types of toys available, types of adult-oriented decorations such as fragile ornaments, general messiness of the setting, the presence of dangerous items, and the overall features of the home. The amount and variety of toys available were not found to be related to any of the study's measures of language or cognitive development. However, other aspects of the home environment were. Children who obtained higher developmental scores on the language and cognitive tests than did age-mates were in situations where the part of the home set aside for the program:

- was safe;

- was relatively neat and orderly;

- was arranged for children; and

- contained few adult-oriented decorations.

Howes (1983) found that child care providers looking after children between age 18 and 22 months who were working in space that was designated for children and safe were less likely to be restrictive or negative than were providers working in space that was unsafe and/or adult-oriented. In addition, they were more likely to be responsive and to engage in activities that would stimulate the children's social development.

The different impact of different types of toys and equipment

Studies indicate that a child's activities can be influenced by the toys and equipment that are available. In a study of 40 children ranging in age from 18 to 22 months, Howes & Rubenstein (1981) found that, in centers, the highest level of interactive play with peers occurred around large non-portable objects such as a climbing apparatus. Children in home-based care, who had less access to such equipment, showed higher levels of interactive play when they were allowed freedom of movement along halls or between connecting rooms. Smith & Connolly (1980) found that three- and four-year-olds in nursery schools were more socially interactive when only large play equipment was available than they were when there were both large pieces of equipment and small toys.

Two center-based studies (Henrickson et al., 1981; Quilitch & Risley, 1973) found that among preschoolers:

◆ children were more apt to play alone if the toys available were mainly things like puzzles, peg boards, lego, play-dough, or tinker toys; and

◆ sharing behavior was associated with balls, puppet stages, dress-up materials, and "housekeeping corners".

What predicts the physical environment?

No research has been done to specifically examine what predicts the physical environment in an early childhood program. An adequate level of funding is obviously required to purchase large pieces of equipment and to design the type of child care or school environment referred to by Moore (1986) as a "well-defined behavior setting". However, the environment also depends on the awareness of staff about what is important in an early childhood setting and their creativity in establishing such an environment. For example, partitioning a large space can be done with little money by using portable office partitions or shelving.

In home-based child care, it is difficult to know if the positive adult behaviors and child development reported by Clarke-Stewart & Gruber

(1984) and Howes (1983) resulted from the characteristics of the environment or whether the environment was a result of the characteristics of the caregiver. It is possible that some caregivers have a psychological predisposition to be responsive to children. Such people might also spontaneously arrange that part of their home being used for child care so that it was child-safe and child-friendly.

Implications for practice

The above studies suggest:

◆ the value in center-based and school-based programs of small activity areas and the provision of different sized spaces for different types of activity;

◆ the value in home-based child care of an area designated and arranged for the use of the children and from which have been removed any dangerous or fragile items that might encourage caregiver restrictiveness; and

◆ the need to provide the types of toys and equipment likely to encourage peer interaction. Peer relationship skills are developed through interaction with other children. This observation suggests that limits should be imposed on the amount of time spent watching television or videotapes, or playing computer games. These are all activities that tend to discourage peer interaction and may be used by some children to avoid contact with other children.

◆ ◆ ◆ ◆ Summary

As discussed in this chapter, the involvement of the parent and various aspects of the daily environment have a direct effect on the child's well-being and development. These relationships are illustrated in Fig. 5.1 on page 64.

Figure 5.1

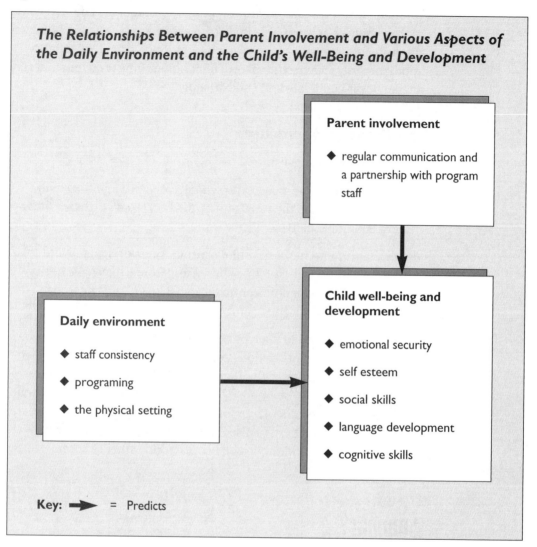

The Relationships Between Parent Involvement and Various Aspects of the Daily Environment and the Child's Well-Being and Development

Parent involvement

◆ regular communication and a partnership with program staff

Daily environment

◆ staff consistency

◆ programing

◆ the physical setting

Child well-being and development

◆ emotional security

◆ self esteem

◆ social skills

◆ language development

◆ cognitive skills

Key: ➡ = Predicts

6 The Structural Features of Quality

The *structural features* of an early childhood program are those features that can be regulated, for example, the staff-to-child ratio and group size. If, as already indicated, the relationship between the adult and child is the most important aspect of an early childhood program, what is the role of the structural features? Research indicates that they support and encourage positive interaction between adults and children and the provision of developmentally appropriate programming. This chapter discusses the research findings related to each of the following six structural features:

- provisions for health;

- the staff-to-child ratio;

- group or classroom size;

- program size;

- density, that is, the number of children in a given space; and

- staff education.

For each feature, the research findings are presented first, then implications for practice are identified.

Provisions for Health

Research findings

Young children are vulnerable to infections because of their immature immune systems. Their exposure to various types of germs and viruses is increased when they have regular contact with a group of other young children. Because of this, preschool-age children in early childhood programs may be more vulnerable to diarrhea and hepatitis than their home-reared peers (Hayes et al., 1990).

Research studies indicate that the extent to which diarrhea or hepatitis actually occur in early childhood programs depends on:

◆ the extent to which the adults are conscientious about hand washing and other sanitary procedures (Black et al., 1981; Gehlbach et al., 1973);

◆ whether or not the same adult diapers children and prepares food (Halder & McFarland, 1986; Lemp et al., 1984). The likelihood of diarrhea and hepatitis is increased when the same person does both activities;

◆ center size. A small center has a greatly reduced risk of infectious disease (Halder et al., 1982; Pickering & Woodward, 1982). The risk of hepatitis outbreaks has been found to rise sharply in child care centers with more than 50 children (Silva, 1980); and

◆ group size (Pickering et al., 1981). Experience suggests that a group size of more than four children under age three is associated with increased incidence of diarrhea, hepatitis, respiratory infection, and influenza.

Black et al. (1981), in an experiment conducted in four ordinary community child care centers in the United States, were able to demonstrate a 50 percent decrease in diarrhea when child and adult hand washing was rigorously enforced.

Implications for practice

Klein (1986, page 12), from the Department of Pediatrics at Boston University School of Medicine, notes that:

> hand washing is the single most important technique for prevention of gastrointestinal and many respiratory infections. Compulsory hand washing after handling infants, blowing noses, changing diapers, and using toilet facilities should be expected of every caregiver.

Both the American Academy of Pediatrics (1992) and the Canadian Paediatric Society (1992), have produced very detailed manuals specifying the elements of good practice as they relate to provisions for health and safety in early childhood programs. Their recommendations include:

◆ having written policies and procedures covering hygiene practices such as: hand washing, general cleaning, sanitation of toys and equipment, safe food preparation and storage, and criteria for exclusion and re-admission of children or staff members who have a communicable illness;

◆ requiring children to have a written health evaluation completed prior to admission, and that this evaluation include information about the child's current health status and immunization record;

◆ the sharing with all staff of relevant information regarding children's allergies and/or other medical conditions;

◆ staff training in: daily health screening of all children, hygiene procedures, cleaning and sanitation procedures, documentation of illness and injury, administration of medicine to children, informing parents of a child's illness or injury, and when to inform the local public health agency about an infection in the program;

◆ education of staff, parents, and children about the transmission, prevention, recognition, and management of infections, and about good health and dental practices;

◆ assignment of a consistent person (a primary care provider) to each child who is not yet toilet trained to reduce the number of possible routes of transmission of infections; and

◆   a diapering and hand washing area that is physically separate from the food preparation area and not used for any other purpose.

Both manuals make recommendations regarding basic safety and injury prevention.

◆ ◆ ◆ ◆ The Staff-to-Child Ratio

The number of children per staff member is referred to as the staff-to-child ratio. Research shows that this has a definite impact on both adult behavior and child functioning.

Research findings

Adult behavior

Center-based child care

Howes et al. (1992) examined the relationship in 227 centers in five different states between different staff-to-adult ratios for children of different ages and:

◆   **appropriate caregiving.** This phrase represented the score obtained from a group of items from the *Early Childhood Environment Rating Scale* (Harms & Clifford, 1980) for preschoolers or the *Infant-Toddler Environment Rating Scale* (Harms & Clifford, 1986) for younger children. The items from the scales pertained to the interaction between the adult and child, supervision, discipline practices, and health and safety practices; and

◆   **developmentally appropriate activity.** This phrase represented the score obtained from a group of items from the two above-noted Harms & Clifford scales pertaining to the extent to which furnishing, the arrangement of the physical space, the toys and equipment, and the program policies are appropriate for the age of the children being served.

Table 6.1 provides a summary of the findings from this study. It shows that the percentage of children not receiving appropriate caregiving, as defined above, increased as the number of children per adult increased. This held true across all three age groups.

The table also shows that the percentage of children not receiving developmentally appropriate activities, as defined above, tended to increase with an increase in the number of children per adult. The significant increase in the percentage of children not receiving appropriate caregiving and not receiving developmentally appropriate activities when above a ratio of 1:3 for infants, 1:4 for toddlers, and 1:8 for preschoolers, should be noted. This suggests that the ratios of 1:3, 1:4, and 1:8 for the three age groups respectively may be thresholds for staff-to-child ratios that separate quality programs from other programs.

Table 6.1

The Relationship Between Staff-to-Child Ratio, Appropriate Caregiving, and Developmentally Appropriate Activity

Staff-to-child ratio by age	Percentage of children not receiving appropriate caregiving	Percentage of children not receiving developmentally appropriate activities
Infants (0–24 months)		
– 1:3 or less	10%	7%
– 1:3 or 4	45%	50%
– more than 1:4	57%	46%
Toddlers (25–36 months)		
– 1:4 or less	4%	2%
– 1:4 to 1:6	26%	41%
– more than 1:6	39%	42%
Preschoolers (37–54 months)		
– 1:8 or less	9%	7%
– 1:8 or 1:9	52%	50%
– more than 1:9	54%	50%

Source: Howes et al., 1992.

Six studies from the United States, three from England, one from Canada, and one from Sweden illustrate the impact of the staff-to-child ratio on adult behavior in *center-based* programs. These studies involved infants, toddlers, and preschoolers. A *small* number of children per adult has been found to be associated with:

◆ adults who are sensitive and responsive to the child (Howes, 1983; Howes & Rubenstein, 1985; Whitebook et al., 1990); and

◆ adults who engage in more social, and/or verbal, and/or cognitive stimulation with the child than do adults responsible for more children (Biemiller et al., 1976; Howes, 1983; Palmerus, 1991; Ruopp et al., 1979; Sylva et al. 1980).

A *large* number of children per adult in center-based programs is associated with:

◆ a higher percentage of caregiver time spent in controlling the children, and a resultant smaller percentage of time spent in social stimulation or teaching (Biemiller et al., 1976; Field, 1980; Melhuish et al., 1990b; Ruopp et al., 1979; Smith & Connolly, 1986; Syvla et al. 1980);

◆ adults who are detached or restrictive (Howes et al., 1988; Howes et al., 1992; Smith & Connolly, 1986; Whitebook et al., 1990); and

◆ fewer individual contacts between child and caregiver than occurs in situations where each adult is responsible for fewer children (Biemiller et al., 1976; Shapiro, 1975).

An exception to the above, was the finding by Ruopp et al. (1979) that staff-to-child ratios varying from 1:5 to 1:10 had no significant impact on adult behavior when *preschoolers* were involved. This is in contrast to the findings of Smith & Connolly (1986) studying ratios of between 1:4 to 1:14 and children of the same age. The difference in findings may reflect the relatively large difference between a staff-to-child ratio of 1:10 and one of 1:14 for preschoolers. The ratio of 1:10 is only one child more than the ratio of 1:9 identified as acceptable for four-, five-, and six-year-olds by both the United States' National Academy of Early Childhood Programs (1984) and the Canadian Child Care Federation (1993).

It is harder to explain why Howes et al. (1992) found such a large difference in adult behavior with *preschoolers* between a staff-to-child ratio of 1:9 versus one of 1:8 (see Table 6.1), while Ruopp et al. report no significant differences in adult behavior for ratios between 1:5 and 1:10. It is possible that the Howes study was more sensitive to picking up adult behaviors. It used a well-established observation instrument, namely the *Early Childhood Environment Rating Scale* (Harms & Clifford, 1980), which is known to be reliable. In contrast, Ruopp et al. counted the number of times specific behaviors were observed. This method may not have been as sensitive in identifying the subtleties of the interactions between the children and adults. Therefore, it is still probable that a ratio of 1:8 or 1:9 is the desirable level for preschoolers.

Home-based child care

Two studies from the United States have examined the impact of ratio on *toddlers* in h*ome-based child care* (Howes, 1983; Howes & Rubenstein, 1985). Both found that a large number of toddlers per caregiver was associated with caregivers who were restrictive. The ratios in these studies were one caregiver for two to six children.

Child behavior

As might be expected, fewer children per adult is associated with positive child development and behavior. More children per adult is associated with child behavior that is undesirable. These findings are consistent across the board with *infants, toddlers,* and *preschoolers,* and in several center-based studies done in the United States, one in Bermuda (Phillips et al., 1987; Schwarz, 1983), and one in New Zealand (Smith et al., 1989).

When there are *fewer* children per adult, children:

- ◆ engage in higher rates of focused behavior and lower rates of unoccupied behavior (Holloway & Reichhart-Erikson, 1988; Vandell & Powers, 1983);

- ◆ show less aggression towards other children (Smith et al., 1989);

- ◆ are rated as more considerate of others (Phillips et al., 1987);

- ◆ are better able to regulate their own behavior (Howes & Olenick, 1986); and

◆ show higher levels of verbal communication skills (Howes & Rubenstein, 1985).

Programs where there is a *large* number of children per adult have been found to be associated with *preschoolers* who have a short attention span and poor verbal skills relative to age-mates in other programs (Schwarz, 1983). *Infants* in such situations have been found to be apathetic and show obvious distress, such as significant amounts of crying (Ruopp et al., 1979).

The only exception to the finding that large numbers of children per adult is associated with undesirable child behavior is a study by Clarke-Stewart & Gruber (1984). They found that two- and three-year-olds in centers with a larger number of children per caregiver were more cooperative with adults and peers than children in centers with smaller staff-to-child ratios. However, the range of ratios in this study was 1:4 to 1:6 for three-year-olds. These ratios are within the standards for this age group recommended by both the United States' National Academy of Early Childhood Programs (1984) and the Canadian Child Care Federation (1993). Both organizations recommend a ratio no higher than 1:6. Studies finding a negative impact on children arising from the staff-to-child ratio all had ratios exceeding those recommended for the age group in question.

Implications for practice

The research clearly indicates that the staff-to-child ratio has a definite impact on both adult behavior and child well-being and development. This is not surprising. Child development is fostered when there is frequent and personal positive interaction between the adult and child. The adult who is responsible for too many children, given their age, can do little more than attend to their physical needs and safety. He or she is also likely to be under significant job-related stress, which increases the probability of harshness and restrictiveness. The study by Howes et al. (see Table 6.1) gives an indication of optimal staff-to-child ratios.

Group or Classroom Size

Research findings

Adult behavior

Center-based child care

Howes et al. (1992), in their study of 227 centers in five different states, also examined the impact of different group or classroom sizes and the extent to which there was appropriate caregiving and developmentally appropriate activity. Their findings are illustrated by Table 6.2. The table shows that the percentage of children not receiving appropriate caregiving and not receiving developmentally appropriate activities generally increased with the increase in group size. The exception is in the infant group where children in groups of 6 to 12 were less likely to receive appropriate caregiving than those in groups with 12 or more children. The researchers do not provide information linking the staff-to-child ratio with the different sized infant groups. The ratio could make a difference. For example, it is possible that each caregiver was responsible for fewer infants in groups of more than 12 infants than was the situation in groups of 6 to 12. If this was so, the caregivers in the larger groups would be in a better position than those in the smaller groups to provide appropriate caregiving.

The American National Day Care Study (Ruopp et al., 1979), which involved 1,800 children from 64 centers, found that for *preschoolers*, class size was the single most important determinant of children's experience. In groups of 12 or less, staff were more actively involved with the children (for example, questioning, responding, praising, or comforting) and spent a lower percentage of their time in straight monitoring or in conversation with other adults than did staff in groups of 24 or more. The benefit of smaller groups was observed even when the staff-to-child ratio was constant. Groups of 12 to 14 children with two adults (ratio 1:6 or 1:7) had better average outcomes than groups of 24 to 28 children with four staff (ratio also 1:6 or 1:7). Kontos & Fiene (1987), also in the United States, found that smaller groups of *preschoolers* were associated with adults who obtained higher scores

Table 6.2

The Relationship Between Group or Classroom Size, Appropriate Caregiving, and Developmentally Appropriate Activity

Group or classroom size by age	Percentage of children not receiving appropriate caregiving	Percentage of children not receiving developmentally appropriate activities
Infants (0–24 months)		
– 6 or fewer children	11%	11%
– 6 to 12 children	32%	32%
– 12 or more children	13%	54%
Toddlers (25–36 months)		
– 12 or fewer children	18%	4%
– 12 to 18 children	22%	37%
– 18 or more children	58%	50%
Preschoolers (37–54 months)		
– 18 or fewer children	9%	6%
– 18 or more children	18%	50%

Source: Howes et al., 1992.

on an observation scale rating them on behaviors such as responsiveness.

Group size in center-based programs has also been found to have an impact with *infants* and *toddlers*. *Larger* groups are associated with adults who:

◆ show higher rates of behaviors that have been shown by research to have a detrimental impact on children's development, for example, restrictiveness (Allhusen & Cochran, 1991; Howes, 1983; Howes & Rubenstein, 1985); and

◆ engage in less social and language stimulation with the children (Howes & Rubenstein, 1985; Ruopp et al., 1979).

Home-based child care

Studies from the United States demonstrate that group size also has an impact on *home-based child care*. *Large* groups are associated with adults who:

◆ show higher rates of behaviors that have been shown by research to have a detrimental impact on children's development, for example, detachment and restrictiveness (Howes, 1983; Howes & Rubenstein, 1985); and

◆ provide less social and other forms of stimulation for the children (Fosburg, 1981; Howes, 1983; Stith & Davis, 1984).

Child behavior

Center-based child care

Research from the United States and from England has found that in *center-based* child care, children in *small* groups, when compared to same-age children in larger groups:

◆ were more actively involved in classroom activities (Ruopp et al., 1979; Smith & Connolly, 1986). This is considered desirable because it increases the child's opportunities for skill development;

◆ showed lower rates of crying and other distress behavior (Howes & Rubenstein, 1985; Ruopp et al., 1979);

◆ were more cooperative with others (Ruopp et al., 1979), and showed better understanding of acceptable social behavior (Clarke-Stewart & Gruber, 1984; Holloway & Reichhart-Erikson, 1988); and

◆ showed greater improvement on tests to measure reading readiness (Ruopp et al., 1979).

In contrast, Kontos & Fiene (1987) report that group size had no impact on the preschoolers in their study. However, there was little variation in group size in their sample. Kontos & Fiene did find that centers with small group sizes obtained higher scores on the *Early Childhood Environment Rating Scale* (Harms & Clifford, 1980). This indicates that these centers had higher global ratings of quality.

Home-based child care

Three studies conducted in the United States indicate that *large* groups also have a negative impact on *toddlers'* behavior in *home-based child care*. The national study done by Fosburg (1981) found that toddlers in large groups spent more time in observation than they did in involvement in activities when compared with age-mates in smaller groups. Clarke-Stewart (1987) reports that children in a group of more than five showed lower social competence with unknown peers than did children in groups of two to four. Howes & Rubenstein (1985) found less crying and higher rates of playing and talking among children in small groups.

Implications for practice

Group size is important for a variety of reasons, for example:

♦ moderate-sized or small groups simultaneously permit children to have a choice of partners while protecting them from overstimulation (Howes, 1987); and

♦ small groups make it easier for the adult to have true verbal exchange with the children, to interact with them as individuals, and to spend a smaller proportion of their time in routines or behavior management (Hayes et al., 1990).

Again, the study by Howes et al. (1992), see Table 6.2, suggests appropriate group sizes for various ages.

♦ ♦ ♦ ♦ Program Size

Research findings

Research from the United States has consistently found that large programs are more likely to be associated with adult behavior known to impede children's development, and with less positive outcomes for children, than are small programs.

Large programs, especially those with over 60 children, have been found to:

◆ be more vulnerable to outbreaks of diarrhea or hepatitis (Halder et al., 1982; Pickering & Woodward, 1982; Silva, 1980); and

◆ have staff with higher rates of undesirable behaviors, such as restrictiveness (Kontos & Fiene, 1987; Prescott et al., 1967).

Clarke-Stewart & Gruber (1984) found that two- and three-year-olds in *large* centers tended to do less well on measures of social competence than age-mates in smaller programs.

Implications for practice

The above research findings suggest that an early childhood program much in excess of 60 children is vulnerable to being too impersonal and regimented. Prescott et al. (1967) observe that the sheer size and complexity of larger centers makes it necessary for groups of children and staff to arrive in designated places or participate in specific activities on schedule so as not to hold up other groups. They suggest that sensitive, responsive caregivers find such regimentation unpleasant and tend to leave. As a result, large centers eventually accumulate a staff of "rule enforcers".

Density

Density refers to the space per child, usually expressed in terms of the square feet per individual. Several studies from the United States, one from England (Smith & Connolly, 1986), and one from the U.S. Virgin Islands (Perry, 1977) indicate that a large number of children in relatively little space has a negative impact on both adult and child behavior.

Research findings

Conditions of *high density*, that is, a large number of children in the space, have been found to be associated with:

- higher rates of adult controlling and restricting behavior (Perry, 1977);

- lower rates of adult and child interaction (Vandell & Powers, 1983); and

- children who engage in aimless wandering, and/or show lower amounts of cooperative play with peers, and/or are more aggressive (Holloway & Reichhart-Erikson, 1988; Phyfe-Perkins, 1979; Rohe & Nuffer, 1977; Shapiro, 1975; Smith & Connolly, 1986; Vandell & Powers, 1983).

Implications for practice

Research shows that the negative impact of a large number of children for the space available can be reduced by:

- adding partitions to divide the space into smaller areas (Field, 1980; Holloway & Reichhart-Erikson, 1988; Rohe & Nuffer, 1977); and

- ensuring there are plenty of toys and pieces of equipment to reduce the need for children to be in competition for them (Prescott, 1981; Smith & Connolly, 1986). Prescott (1981) suggests that it is important, even with very young children, to ensure that there are opportunities for privacy, for example, a screened-off space. High density situations tend to involve high levels of noise and other stimulation. Some children are more prone to being negatively affected by high levels of stimulation than are other children. Children with this sensitivity need to be able to remove themselves from a situation when they begin to feel stressed.

◆ ◆ ◆ ◆ Staff Education

There are four aspects to consider in regard to staff education.

1. Does formal education, that is, the number of years of schooling, and/or education related specifically to child development or early childhood education, make a difference to the child's daily experience or development?

2. If years of formal education and/or training related specifically to child development or early childhood education does make a difference, which is the better predictor of children's well-being and development?

3. Does child age or special need make a difference in the type of adult preparation that is desirable?

4. Is special preparation desirable for supervisors and directors?

Research findings

The impact of education

Center-based and school-based programs

Research from the United States, Canada, and Bermuda has found that staff who have some college education in any discipline and/or post-secondary school training in child development or early childhood education:

◆ show higher rates of positive adult behaviors, such as responsiveness, encouragement of the child's efforts, and social stimulation, than do staff with only a high-school diploma or less (Arnett, 1989; Berk, 1985; Friesen, 1992; Howes, 1983; Ruopp et al., 1979; Whitebook et al., 1990); and

◆ are more likely to provide developmentally appropriate activities for the children (Howes, 1983; Ruopp et al., 1979; Whitebook et al., 1990).

Children whose staff have either post-secondary school education or education specific to child development or early childhood education receive higher scores on various measures of child development than do children whose staff do not have this educational background (Clarke-Stewart & Gruber, 1984; Howes & Olenick, 1986; Ruopp et al., 1979; Vandell & Powers, 1983).

Home-based child care

Research from the United States and Canada also indicates that *home-based child care providers* with some college education and/or post-secondary school training in child development or early childhood education show higher rates of positive caregiver behaviors (Fosburg, 1981; Howes, 1983; Jones & Meisels, 1987; Pence & Goelman, 1991; Stuart & Pepper, 1988).

Clarke-Stewart & Gruber (1984), in the United States, report that higher caregiver education is associated with children who show better social competence with adults.

The impact of training related to the provision of an early childhood program

Center-based child care

Some of the studies cited in the previous section did not explore whether the desirable impact of post-secondary school education was due to the level of education itself or to having specific training related to early childhood programs. Two large American multi-site *center-based* studies have examined the issue of formal education versus specific training related to child development or the provision of an early childhood program.

The National Day Care Study (Ruopp et al., 1979) involved 1,800 *infants, toddlers*, and *preschoolers* from 64 child care centers in three large cities. It found that:

◆ caregivers with post-secondary school education *related* to child care were significantly more likely than staff with post-secondary school education unrelated to child care to show behaviors found by research to facilitate child development, for example, positive adult interaction; and

◆ the children in the care of adults with post-secondary school education *related* to child care showed greater cooperative behavior, greater task persistence, higher levels of language skills, and higher levels of general knowledge than age-mates whose caregivers had post-secondary school education unrelated to early childhood programs.

The National Child Care Staffing Study (Whitebook et al., 1990) involved 227 child care centers in five cities and children from *infancy to age six*. This study found that people with post-secondary school training in early childhood education provided children in their care with more appropriate caregiving for their age. The measure of appropriate caregiving included things like the extent to which the adult showed behaviors known to facilitate child development, the degree to which the adult's supervision of the child was appropriate for the child's developmental level, and the extent to which overall programing was age-appropriate.

Snider & Fu (1990) tested 73 child care providers for *three-, four-, and five- year-olds* on their knowledge of developmentally appropriate practice. The subjects had one of the following: high school diploma only, child development associate credential[1], an associate degree in child development or early childhood education, a masters degree in child development or early childhood education, or some other training or degree. They found that people who had training in child development and/or early childhood education obtained better scores than did caregivers with other types of degrees or only a high school diploma.

Home-based child care

Studies involving *home-based child care providers* conducted in both the United States and Canada also demonstrate the value of post-secondary school training in child development or early childhood education. In the United States, Fischer & Eheart (1991) found that the provider's training in child care was the single best predictor of observed caregiving practices. It discriminated between care providers at a statistically significant level and was responsible for 52 percent of the differences in practice observed among them. Howes (1983) found that providers with training in early childhood education or a related field were more likely to be responsive, to play with the children, and to provide them with social stimulation. These findings are similar to those of Fosburg (1981) in the 352 homes studied in the National Day Care Home Study.

Four American studies have demonstrated a positive impact on overall quality, as measured by the *Family Day Care Rating Scale* (Harms & Clifford, 1989), after in-service training (Jones & Meisels, 1987; Kontos, 1988; Nelson, 1989; and Ungaretti, 1987). In all the studies, except that by Kontos (1988), the difference in before- and after-training scores was statistically significant. A fifth study found that children being cared for by home-based providers who received ten months' of weekly training sessions made greater gains on standard tests of language and cognitive skills than did children in a comparison group where the providers did not receive training (Goodman & Andrews, 1981).

The Canadian research supports the findings of the above American studies. Both Pence & Goelman (1991) and Stuart & Pepper (1988) found that caregivers with post-secondary school training related to early childhood education obtained statistically significant higher scores on the *Day Care Home Environment Rating Scale* (Harms et al., 1988) than did providers whose post-secondary school education was unrelated to child care provision.

The impact of age or special need

In a survey of 52 key child care researchers and academics across the United States and Canada, Doherty (1991) found a remarkably consistent opinion that:

◆ adults looking after infants and toddlers in a group setting need specific training related to this age group, and the training requirements are different from what is required to provide quality programing for preschoolers; and

◆ adults working in programs for school-age children over age six require training that focuses on child development in the period between age 6 and 12, and that recognizes the differences in developmental tasks and issues for 6- to 9- year-olds and 10- to 12-year-olds.

The need for specific training for people working with children who have special needs is discussed in Chapter 11.

Preparation requirements for supervisors and directors

Jorde-Bloom (1989) conducted a study in Illinois in which she examined the training and education needs of child care center directors through a combination of:

◆ a questionnaire sent to 990 directors of licensed centers;

- site visits to 103 programs. These visits included the administration of part of the scale used to evaluate centers applying for accreditation by the United States' National Academy of Early Childhood Education; and

- a questionnaire sent to 89 experts in early childhood education.

Seventy-six percent of the directors and 87 percent of the experts stated that graduation from a post-secondary school program in early childhood education, plus courses in the administration of a child care center, should be a pre-requisite to becoming a director. They also agreed that prior experience as a frontline caregiver was essential.

In the Jorde-Bloom study, the director's formal education level, that is, university degree or no university degree, was the strongest predictor of quality as measured by the National Academy of Early Childhood Education scale. However, there was also a statistically significant relationship (though not as strong) between:

- quality and specialized training in early childhood education; and

- quality and training in the administration of a child care center.

Many of the directors' university degrees were in early childhood education. Therefore, it is impossible to know whether the association between the director having a university degree, and a rating of high quality, was a result of having a degree in and of itself. It could also have been the result of post-secondary school education related to the provision of child care.

Implications for practice

There appears to be agreement that quality early childhood programs are associated with staff who have post-secondary school education. However, there has been some debate in the professional literature as to whether the sheer amount of education or the content of the education is the better predictor of quality. A review of the research literature indicates that education in child development or early childhood education is the crucial factor. Experts suggest that it is also important to prepare workers for the different developmental tasks and needs of children of different ages, and the unique necessities of children with special needs. Additional training in management appears to be desirable for a supervisor or program director.

Most skilled jobs, for example, nursing, assume that certain knowledge and skills are necessary and that specific education is required before beginning work in the field. Usually job-related skills are learned in a formalized education program that is then supplemented by supervised practice in a work site. The provision of an early childhood program also involves a set of learnable skills. Therefore, training to do the work increases the likelihood that it will be done well, that is, that the adult will provide an experience that will foster the child's well-being and development. The interaction between the adult and child is the most important aspect of the child's experience. Obviously, the quality of this interaction is not *solely* dependent on the adult's training and education. Personal characteristics probably play a role, and, as will be discussed in Chapter 7, research has shown that the characteristics of the adult work environment influence adult behavior. Nevertheless, responsiveness, positive adult interaction, the use of true verbal exchange, and developmentally appropriate practice are all behaviors that can be learned in an education program and practiced in supervised settings.

❖ ❖ ❖ ❖ Summary

As suggested at the beginning of this chapter, structural factors support and encourage positive interaction between adults and children. This, in turn, increases the likelihood of the child's well-being and development. These relationships are illustrated in Fig. 6.1 on page 85.

Notes

[1] The United States' Child Development Associate (CDA) Program has established certain knowledge and skills considered to be necessary for competent child care provision. This forms the basis for non-college training courses that can lead to being granted a child development associate credential. The associate degree in child development or early childhood education is usually received after completing two years of community college.

Figure 6.1

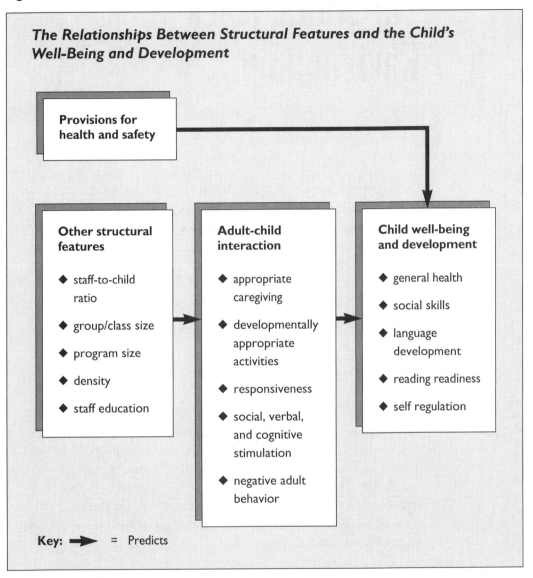

The Relationships Between Structural Features and the Child's Well-Being and Development

Provisions for health and safety

Other structural features

◆ staff-to-child ratio

◆ group/class size

◆ program size

◆ density

◆ staff education

Adult-child interaction

◆ appropriate caregiving

◆ developmentally appropriate activities

◆ responsiveness

◆ social, verbal, and cognitive stimulation

◆ negative adult behavior

Child well-being and development

◆ general health

◆ social skills

◆ language development

◆ reading readiness

◆ self regulation

Key: ➡ = Predicts

The Adult Work Environment

The key element in an early childhood program, the amount and type of interaction between the adult and child, is affected by how the adult feels about his or her job. Research indicates that the adult work environment helps determine job satisfaction. Job satisfaction or dissatisfaction, in turn, has an impact on the adult's behavior and, through this, an impact on the child's well-being and development. The specific aspects of the adult environment in early childhood programs that have been found to predict the extent of job satisfaction are:

◆ salaries and benefits;

◆ general working conditions; and

◆ the administrative style of the program's senior staff.

This chapter discusses the research findings related to each of these three aspects of the adult work environment, the impact of job dissatisfaction, and some implications for practice. There appears to be no research that has examined the impact of the work environment on job satisfaction among home-based child care providers. However, the value of providing support services for this group has been documented and is discussed in Chapter 8.

The Research Findings

Salaries and benefits

The American National Child Care Staffing Study (Whitebook et al., l990), which involved 1,309 child care center caregivers, found that the best predictor of job satisfaction was salary. Higher salaries were associated with viewing child care as a career and with higher job commitment. Staff earning salaries at the lower end of the range left their jobs at twice the rate of those whose salaries were higher. The findings relating salary to job satisfaction and turnover rates are similar to those from earlier surveys done in the United States (Hartman & Pearce, 1989; Kontos & Stremmel, 1988; Whitebook at al., 1982) and a more recent study by Stremmel (1991).

Canadian research supports the above findings. A recent study involving all ten provinces, the Yukon, and the Northwest Territories obtained information from 2,383 frontline staff and 502 directors representing 969 child care centers (Canadian Child Care Federation/ Canadian Day Care Advocacy Association, 1992). Fifty-two percent of the respondents expressed dissatisfaction with their current salary and benefit package and 20 percent indicated that they were thinking of leaving the child care field because of the low salary levels. An earlier survey that also involved all the provinces and both territories found that 24 percent of the 335 respondents stated they intended to leave the child care field and cited salary levels as the primary reason (Schom-Moffat, 1984).

Salary levels also have a direct impact on the children. In the United States, Whitebook et al. (1990) found that child care staff earning salaries at the higher end of the range worked in centers where there were higher levels of developmentally appropriate activities for all age groups (infant, toddler, and preschool).

General working conditions

The extent to which adult needs are met

Phillips et al. (1991) did a special analysis of the data from the American National Child Care Staffing Study (Whitebook et al., 1990) to examine the impact of the adult work environment. They found that job satisfaction among staff working with preschoolers was predicted by the extent to which adult needs were met as measured by the *Early Childhood Environment Rating Scale* (Harms & Clifford, 1980). The adult needs measured by this scale are: the availability of a staff lounge and separate staff restroom, the availability of storage space for personal belongings, the availability of a staff meeting area with appropriate adult furniture, the provision of opportunities for professional growth and development, and the provision of opportunities for exchange of information with parents.

The staff-to-child ratio

A study involving 83 center-based child care staff in the United States found that staff with more children per caregiver were more dissatisfied with their job (Maslach & Pines, 1977). Similar findings are reported by other more recent American studies involving center-based child care (Kontos & Stremmel, 1988; Whitebook et al., 1982). When asked to make recommendations for improving their jobs, the greatest number (37 percent) of the 40 respondents to the Kontos & Stremmel (1988) survey suggested reducing the number of children for whom they were responsible.

Research conducted in Canada and England supports the American findings. In the recent Canada-wide survey, one of the recommendations most frequently made by frontline staff was to reduce the number of children per caregiver (Canadian Child Care Federation/Canadian Day Care Advocacy Association, 1992). In England, when Smith & Connolly (1986) increased the number of children for whom a caregiver was directly responsible, the caregivers reported their work to be less satisfying.

Paid preparation time

Having time for preparation during the paid hours of work was the second best predictor of job satisfaction found by the American National Child Care Staffing Study (Whitebook et al., 1990). Paid preparation time was associated with feelings of having a good relationship with the supervisor or director and overall satisfaction with the center's working conditions. In a recent Canadian survey, respondents' third most frequently made recommendation was to provide paid preparation time (Canadian Child Care Federation/Canadian Day Care Advocacy Association, 1992).

The impact on children

General staff working conditions also have a direct impact on the children. Phillips et al. (1991) found that the adequacy with which adult needs were met, as measured by the *Early Childhood Environment Rating Scale* (Harms & Clifford, 1980), was the second most important predictor (after salary) of the extent to which developmentally appropriate activities were provided for the children.

The administrative style

Three studies from the United States and one from Canada have found that the way in which a child care center is operated has an impact on the job satisfaction felt by its staff members. In the United States, job satisfaction has been found to be associated with:

◆ provision for frontline staff to have input into center policy and program development (Maslach & Pines, 1977; Whitebook et al., 1982);

◆ regular provision of a short break in the morning and afternoon (Maslach & Pines, 1977); and

◆ regular staff meetings to discuss individual children and/or work issues (Maslach & Pines, 1977).

Job dissatisfaction and stated intention to leave the center has been found to be associated with perceived lack of feedback and support from the center director (Stremmel, 1991).

In the recent Canada-wide survey involving 2,383 frontline staff, providing more opportunities for frontline staff to be involved in decision making and a short break in the morning and afternoon were two of the most frequently mentioned recommendations made by respondents (Canadian Child Care Federation/Canadian Day Care Advocacy Association, 1992).

The Impact of Job Satisfaction and Job Dissatisfaction

Studies conducted in the United States indicate that adult job satisfaction has a direct impact on children through its influence on adult behavior and an indirect influence through its association with high staff turnover rates.

Adult behavior

Berk (1985) found a statistically significant relationship in twelve programs serving three- to five-year-olds between:

◆ staff satisfaction with salary, working conditions, and employee policies; and

◆ the extent to which staff provided encouragement and guidance to children and activities that would encourage their verbal development. Adults who were dissatisfied with their job tended to be restrictive and controlling with the children.

Phillips et al. (1991) report that in their study of 1,307 caregivers, those who were dissatisfied with their job were more likely to fail to provide developmentally appropriate activities.

Haddock & McQueen (1983) compared 21 employees of various types of children's programs who had been found to be abusive with a matched group of 21 non-abusive staff members. The two groups were matched on age, education, and race in an attempt to remove the possible influence of any of these variables. Using a standard questionnaire completed by the subject, the researchers correctly identified 93 percent of the sample as having, or not having, a history of abusive behavior with children. Haddock & McQueen also examined job satisfaction and found a statistically significant relationship between job dissatisfaction and a history of being abusive. Using the same questionnaire as used by Haddock & McQueen, Atten & Milner (1987) studied 152 staff members in child care centers. They found a positive relationship between job dissatisfaction and a score on the questionnaire that indicated that the person had a high potential for being abusive with children.

The impact of high staff turnover rates

As noted above, both American and Canadian research has found that job dissatisfaction predicts staff turnover. High staff turnover rates have been found to impact on the global quality rating obtained by child care centers, staff behavior, and child well-being and development

Center quality

Phillips et al. (1987), in a study conducted in nine centers in Bermuda, found that centers with low staff turnover rates had the highest total scores on the *Early Childhood Environment Rating Scale* (Harms & Clifford, 1980).

Adult behavior

High rates of staff turnover in child care centers have been found to be associated with:

◆ low rates of interaction between the adult and child (Phillips et al., 1987); and

◆ poor scores on an observation scale of caregiver behavior that measured adult behaviors such as responsiveness (Kontos & Fiene, 1987).

Child well-being and development

In their study of 227 child care centers in the United States, Whitebook et al. (1990) found that children in centers that had experienced high staff turnover in the previous twelve months:

- showed less attachment to their caregivers;

- spent significantly less time engaged in social activities and more time in aimless wandering than did children in centers with lower staff turnover rates;

- had lower developmental levels of play;

- received lower scores on a standard measure of language development than did age-mates in other centers that had experienced lower staff turnover rates; and

- had a lower perception of their own competence.

The national annual staff turnover rate found in this American study was 41 percent. In contrast, the recent Canadian study reported that, on a nation-wide basis, 26 percent of the staff had left their jobs in the one-year period before the information was collected (Canadian Child Care Federation/Canadian Day Care Advocacy Association, 1992).

Implications for Practice

Job satisfaction is predicted by: salaries and benefits, the general working conditions, and the administrative style of the program's senior staff.

Salary is dictated, to a large extent, by the center's budget, as are benefits such as vacation time and paid preparation time. However, as noted by Jorde-Bloom (1988) in her monograph on assessing and improving a center's organizational climate, and by Whitebook et al. (1982), there are several steps a program director can take to improve working conditions and staff members' feelings of being valued. These include:

- providing real opportunities for frontline worker input into policy and program decision making;

- being available when staff want to discuss issues or problems;

- providing opportunities for professional growth (for example, staff training); and

- trying to ensure that staff members have a 15-minute break each morning and afternoon.

◆ ◆ ◆ ◆ The Impact of the Adult Work Environment

As previously discussed in this chapter, various aspects of the adult work environment influence adult behavior which, in turn, influences child well-being and development. These relationships are illustrated in Fig. 7.1.

Figure 7.1

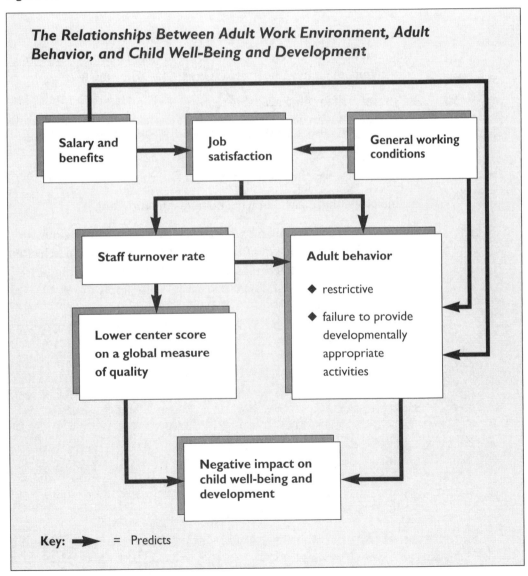

The Relationships Between Adult Work Environment, Adult Behavior, and Child Well-Being and Development

Salary and benefits

Job satisfaction

General working conditions

Staff turnover rate

Adult behavior

◆ restrictive

◆ failure to provide developmentally appropriate activities

Lower center score on a global measure of quality

Negative impact on child well-being and development

Key: ➡ = Predicts

Contextual Factors

Contextual factors are factors outside the individual program that have a direct impact on how the program functions. They include:

◆ the level of funding available to the program;

◆ regulation and its enforcement in the jurisdiction in which the program operates;

◆ agency sponsorship of home-based child care providers; and

◆ auspices, that is, who or what operates the program.

This chapter discusses the research findings for each of these four factors and the relationship of each to quality. While the research cited is specific to child care, it is reasonable to expect that the findings related to funding level and regulation would also apply to kindergarten programs.

◆ ◆ ◆ ◆ Funding

On the basis of the data collected in their survey of 227 child care centers serving children from infancy to age six in five different states, Whitebook et al. (1990, page 112) concluded that:

> better quality centers paid higher wages, had more teachers caring for fewer children, employed better educated and trained staff, had lower staff turnover, and better adult work environments.

As discussed in previous chapters, all the program characteristics listed in the above quote have been found by research to predict child well-being and development. The ability to pay higher wages, to have fewer children per staff member, and to provide a better adult work environment, requires the availability of adequate funding for the program.

In the United States and Canada, most child care is operated by the private sector, that is, voluntary organizations, parents' groups, commercial operators, or employers. In both countries, the majority of regulated child care spaces receive either minimal government funding or none at all. As a result, child care is funded primarily through parent fees. This heavy reliance on parent fees to provide operating funds places child care centers in the difficult position of:

◆ trying to keep fees within a range that parents can afford. This is essential because the program needs a certain level of enrollment in order to meet its basic operating costs; while

◆ trying to pay sufficiently high wages and provide a work environment that will allow the program to attract and retain trained staff.

Quality child care is labor intensive. A relatively large number of staff is required for the number of children in the program to ensure appropriate ratios and group sizes. Surveys in both the United States and Canada have found that non-profit centers allocate about 75 percent of their budget for staff salaries and benefits (Kagan & Newton, 1989; Canadian Child Care Federation/Canadian Day Care Advocacy Association, 1992). In a tight money situation, one of the main ways to control costs is through paying low salaries. In the United States, in 1988, child care staff earned less than half as much as comparably educated women and less than one-third as much as comparably educated men in other fields of work (Whitebook et al., 1990). The situation is similar in Canada. The report of a recent survey noted that, in 1991, the average wage for a warehouse worker, a job requiring less skill and education, was 58 percent more than that of a frontline child care staff person (Canadian Child Care Federation/Canadian Day Care Advocacy Association, 1992). While low staff salaries keep costs down, they increase the likelihood of staff turnover and the likelihood of people leaving the child care field for other types of work. As noted in Chapter 7, high levels of staff turnover have a negative impact on adult behavior with children and on children's development.

◆ ◆ ◆ ◆ Regulation and Its Enforcement

Definition and rationale

The term **"regulation"** refers to the establishment and enforcing of standards for service provision. Standards for child care and for kindergarten typically involve some or all of the structural factors discussed in Chapter 6, namely: provisions for health and safety, the staff-to-child ratio, group and program size, density, and staff training. If child care is government-operated, as it is in most of Western Europe, service regulation is done as part of the administration of the system. In North America, where child care is primarily delivered by voluntary organizations and commercial operators, independent regulation by government is necessary to increase the likelihood that the service will not harm children.

The three components of regulation

A system of regulation includes three components: legislated requirements, program monitoring, and penalties for failure to meet the requirements. It is essential to recognize that:

◆ the legislated requirements represent the *minimum* of what the society in question will tolerate. The extent of the relationship between quality and regulation depends upon the extent to which the requirements extend beyond the threshold of practice that might harm a child; and

◆ regulation can only be effective if there is *both* adequate monitoring of every program and strict enforcement of the required standards.

The following example illustrates the way that the level of the legislated requirements can increase the likelihood of quality programs. If the legislation in one jurisdiction requires a minimum of one frontline staff person with at least two years of post-secondary school training for each class, while the legislation in another jurisdiction only requires that frontline staff have high school graduation, programs in the first jurisdiction will have a larger proportion of staff with two years of training. This will happen because all programs in the first jurisdiction must meet the requirement of one staff person per class who has two years of training. In the second jurisdiction, centers do not have to meet this requirement. The difference in the minimal requirement will influence the likelihood of quality because of the proven association between post-secondary school education related to child care provision and adult behaviors known to facilitate child development.

Adequate monitoring requires properly trained monitors, using a process that is consistent across the jurisdiction, and regular, unannounced visits. The people doing the monitoring need a thorough basis in child development and early childhood programing in order to assess program aspects, for example, the extent to which developmentally appropriate practice is occurring. Basic fairness requires a consistent process so that all programs are assessed using the same criteria. Finally, unannounced visits may provide a more accurate picture of the program because they preclude special arrangements being made by the program on days when a monitoring visit is scheduled.

Enforcement is the final aspect of an effective regulatory system. The level of the minimal requirements, and the frequency of monitoring, will make no difference to quality if violation of the legislated requirements is not addressed. As research from the United States and Canada demonstrates, indicators of poor quality can be found in regulated programs (Fiene & Melnick, 1990; Friesen, 1992; Jorde-Bloom, 1989; Kontos & Fiene, 1987; Kontos & Stremmel, 1998; West, 1988; Whitebook et al., 1990). Therefore, it is obvious that regulation must be supplemented by monitoring and enforcement.

Research on center-based child care programs

When Phillips et al. (1992) did a further analysis of the data from the National Child Care Staffing Study (Whitebook et al., 1990), they found a statistically significant relationship between:

◆ quality as measured by either the *Infant/Toddler Environment Rating Scale* (Harms et al., 1990) or the *Early Childhood Environment Rating Scale* (Harms & Clifford, 1980); and

◆ the level of the regulatory requirements of the state in which the center operated.

Of the five states involved, Massachussetts had the highest requirements for staff-to-child ratio, group size, and staff training. Michigan and Washington closely matched Massachusetts' ratio requirements but either had no standards for group size or staff training or their standards in these areas were lower. Georgia had the lowest requirements, with Arizona having the second lowest. The data analysis found that:

◆ staff in Massachusetts had, on average, significantly more training in early childhood education than did staff in Georgia or Arizona;

◆ infant and toddler classrooms in Massachusetts and Michigan offered significantly more developmentally appropriate activities than did those in Georgia or Washington. Preschool classrooms in Massachusetts offered significantly more developmentally appropriate activities than those offered in any other state;

◆ centers in Massachusetts had, on average, lower staff turnover rates than did centers in either Georgia or Arizona;

◆ the interaction level between adults and children, and the general quality of caregiving, was much lower in Georgia than in any other state; and

◆ staff in Georgia were observed to be significantly more harsh, and significantly less sensitive, with the children than caregivers in any other state.

Research on home-based child care

In the United States, Fosburg (1981) compared regulated homes with unregulated homes on a nation-wide basis. He found that caregivers in unregulated homes spent substantially less time involved with the children than did caregivers in regulated homes. More recently, Galinsky et al. (1994), in a study involving three states, found that regulated providers were:

◆ rated as more sensitive than unregulated providers on a standard scale to measure caregiver sensitivity; and

◆ observed to be more responsive.

In addition, regulated homes were more likely than unregulated homes to provide adequate or good care, as measured by the *Family Day Care Rating Scale* (Harms & Clifford, 1989). Unregulated homes were more likely to provide care that was rated as inadequate by this scale.

Two studies conducted in Canada found that regulated home-based caregivers, as a group, obtained higher scores on the *Day Care Home Environment Rating Scale* (Harms & Clifford, 1983) than did unregulated providers (Goelman & Pence, 1988; Pence & Goelman, 1991). One of the studies also examined children's language development and found that the mean scores on language tests of children in unregulated homes were significantly lower than the mean scores of age-mates in homes that were regulated (Goelman & Pence, 1988).

The impact of regulation

Regulation sets standards for the structural features of a program, that is: basic hygiene and safety, the staff-to-child ratio, group and program size, density, and staff training. While regulation cannot ensure quality, it can, if its requirements are above a minimal level, increase the likelihood that quality will exist.

Sponsorship in Home-Based Child Care Programs

In North America, regulation of home-based child care providers takes one of two forms, as follows:

◆ direct licensing of each individual home by the state, province, or territory in which the home operates; or

◆ regulation through an agency licensed by the state or province to sponsor and monitor a number of homes. In this sponsorship situation, the agency is required to provide regular, on-site supervision of each home, and may also be required to provide training for the child care provider.

Research findings

Four American studies have examined the differences between sponsored and unsponsored home-based child care. Carew (1979), in the course of a lengthy naturalistic observation, found that sponsored caregivers were much more involved with the children, for example, teaching, helping, and offering direction. Toddlers in unsponsored homes spent more time on their own and appeared to be more unhappy than did toddlers in homes that were sponsored. Fosburg (1981) studied unregulated homes, licensed homes, and individual home-based child care providers sponsored by an agency. He found that sponsored caregivers showed the highest rates of interaction with the children and spent more time in activities that would encourage motor and language development than did unregulated or directly licensed caregivers. Fischer & Eheart (1991) reported a significant relationship between affiliation with a support network and desirable caregiver practice as measured by the *Family Day Care Rating Scale* (Harms & Clifford, 1988). However, Fiene & Melnick (1990) found no difference between sponsored and non-sponsored homes on the mean score of the *Family Day Care Rating Scale.* Insufficient information is provided in the report to form an hypothesis as to why this study's findings are not consistent with the findings of other studies.

Research from Canada and Israel supports the American findings. In a study that compared Canadian home-based caregivers who were working independently with sponsored caregivers, Pepper & Stuart (1992) found that the sponsored homes obtained significantly higher ratings on the *Day Care Home Environment Rating Scale* (Harms et al., 1983). Generally, the tone and quality of caregiver and child interaction in the sponsored and non-sponsored homes were the same. However, the sponsored homes obtained substantially better scores on items dealing with health and safety, the arrangement of space, the provision of varied activities, and parent relationships. Rosenthall (1991), in Israel, found that the frequency of individual supervision that a home-based child care provider received from the sponsoring agency (once a week or less frequently) significantly predicted the quality of the interaction between the caregiver and the children for whom she or he was responsible.

The impact of sponsorship

The research findings cited above demonstrate a statistically significant relationship between sponsorship and:

◆ homes with a higher rating on a global measure of quality; and

◆ caregivers who are more likely to be involved with the children and to provide them with stimulating activities.

The reason for the positive impact of sponsorship is not as evident as is the reason for quality being related to adequate funding and to high regulatory standards. Center-based care provides the caregiver with opportunities for regular contact with other adults during the day, the sharing of tasks, and the possibility of assistance from other staff in difficult situations. Home-based child care does not. In addition, some neighborhoods consist primarily of families where the adults work outside the home. As a result, home-based child care providers may be very isolated. Regular visits by sponsoring agency staff may alleviate some of this isolation, thereby improving the provider's work environment.

◆ ◆ ◆ ◆ Auspices

The term **"auspices"** refers to who or what operates the child care program. In North America, child care programs may be operated by a non-profit organization or corporation, such as a parent group or a WYCA, or by a for-profit organization. The category of for-profit organization includes situations where one person operates one program or a number of programs as a business, but may or may not be incorporated, and for-profit corporations with several programs. Sponsored home-based child care providers may be under either non-profit or for-profit auspices.

The operation of, and the provision of public funding to, for-profit child care has been a controversial issue for many years. Child care advocates have consistently taken the position that quality may be sacrificed when a program has to make a profit. This assumes that the requirement of profit-making provides a motivation for cutting costs, for example, having more children per caregiver. Commercial operators with several centers claim that their greater efficiency, such as bulk buying, enables them to provide quality and still make a profit. They also assert that market competition motivates them to keep quality high in order to attract users. Small owner-operators, who may run only one or two programs and function as program directors, resist being classified with large commercial operators. Their position is that they don't make a profit since the funds remaining after covering operating costs are only sufficient to pay the owner-operator's salary at the usual rate for a director position in a non-profit center. The *important* question in this complex debate is whether or not auspices makes a difference in program quality.

Research findings

Quality from a global perspective

Studies from the United States have reported the following:

◆ non-profit centers obtained higher scores on the *Early Childhood Environment Rating Scale* (Harms & Clifford, 1980) or the *Infant/Toddler Environment Rating Scale* (Harms et al., 1990) than did for-profit centers (Fiene & Melnick, 1990; Kontos & Fiene, 1986; Kontos & Stremmel, 1988; Whitebook et al., 1990);

◆ non-profit centers consistently obtained higher scores on the measure used for accreditation by the National Association for the Education of Young Children (Jorde-Bloom, 1989); and

◆ non-profit programs were superior to for-profit programs in regard to the staff-to-child ratio, the overall environment, caregiver encouragement of children, and caregiver appropriate limit setting (Kagan & Newton, 1989).

Canadian studies report similar findings. In a small study involving 45 centers, Friesen (1992) found that:

◆ for-profit centers were significantly more likely to provide a program rated as "poor" by the *Infant/Toddler Environment Rating Scale* (Harms et al., 1990) than were non-profit centers; and

◆ non-profit centers were significantly more likely to provide a program rated as "good" on the *Infant/Toddler Environment Rating Scale* than were for-profit centers.

In a national study involving 927 centers and every province and territory, SPR Associates Inc. (1986) found that non-profit centers tended to be ranked higher than for-profit centers on all ten items on a scale which pertained to enhancing child development. They also tended to receive better ratings in regard to staff-to-child ratios and the quality of the interaction between adults and children, and to have lower staff turnover rates. This study has been criticized because the evaluation of the centers was done by government officials who knew that the purpose of the research was to study the impact of auspices. This knowledge could have introduced a bias into the ratings. Furthermore, there was no independent checking of the government officials' rating by an objective outside person. Its findings are, however, consistent with other research cited above.

Individual indicators of quality

Research in both the United States and Canada has found that non-profit status is associated with: fewer children per caregiver, staff with higher levels of education and more training related to child care, better adult work environments, and lower staff turnover rates, than found in for-profit programs.

The staff-to-child ratio

Two American surveys found that non-profit centers, as a group, had fewer children per caregiver than did for-profit centers (Kagan & Newton, 1989; Whitebook et al., 1990). In Canada, for-profit centers were found to be significantly more often in violation of the staff-to-child ratio required by legislation than were non-profit centers (DeGagné & Gagné, 1988; West, 1988). The study by West is particularly interesting because it found that centers that were officially non-profit, but had an owner-appointed board, were more similar to for-profit centers than to other non-profit centers in terms of the likelihood that they would be in violation of ratio requirements. A third Canadian study found no statistically significant difference in staff-to-child ratios between for-profit and non-profit centers (Friesen, 1992). However, the researcher reported that the non-profit programs tended to have fewer children per caregiver.

Staff education

Large multi-site surveys conducted in both the United States and Canada, as well as a smaller Canadian study, have found that staff in non-profit centers have significantly higher levels of education, as well as more training related to child care, than do their counterparts in for-profit programs (Canadian Child Care Federation/Canadian Day Care Advocacy Association, 1992; Friesen, 1992; Whitebook et al., 1990).

The adult work environment

Whitebook et al. (1990), in their multi-state survey, found that non-profit and church-sponsored centers allocated 62 percent and 63 percent of their budgets, respectively, to salaries and benefits. The same survey found that independent for-profit and chain for-profit centers allocated 49 percent and 41 percent respectively. An analysis of all the data showed that centers allocating a greater share of their funds to salaries and benefits had higher scores on a standard measure of appropriate caregiving and developmentally appropriate activities. The survey also found that non-profit centers provided better working conditions than did for-profit programs at a statistically significant level in all the 12 areas that were examined. In a second American study, Kagan & Newton (1989) found that non-profit centers spent, on average, 75 percent of their funds on staff salaries and benefits in contrast to the 57 percent spent by for-profit centers on the same items.

A recent Canadian nation-wide survey reported that non-profit centers provided higher mean hourly wages, and were significantly more likely to provide staff with paid time for preparation, paid sick leave, paid coffee and lunch breaks, and a variety of other staff benefits than were for-profit centers (Canadian Child Care Federation/ Canadian Day Care Advocacy Association, 1992). These findings echo the findings of another recent Canadian study (Friesen, 1992).

Staff turnover rates

The 227 center American study conducted by Whitebook et al. (1990) found that the annual turnover rate was higher in for-profit than in non-profit centers. The picture in Canada appears to be similar. The 1992 nation-wide study found that staff in non-profit centers had been at the same center for an average of 3.7 years in comparison to 2.9 years for staff in for-profit centers (Canadian Child Care Federation/ Canadian Day Care Advocacy Association). A second study, which examined all the regulated centers in the province of Quebec, found that, in a 12-month period, 35 percent of the for-profit centers had a turnover rate of 40 percent or higher in comparison to a turnover rate of 20 percent in the non-profit centers (DeGagné & Gagné, 1988).

Why does auspices make a difference?

Kagan & Newton (1989) in the United States, and SPR Associates Inc. (1986) in Canada, have both suggested that the differences noted above between for-profit and non-profit centers are a result of the absence of direct government subsidy to for-profit programs. However, in the United States, the 227-center study conducted in five different states found that for-profit centers tended to provide lower quality programs whether or not they received government funding (Whitebook et al., 1990). Two Canadian studies, both conducted at a time when the respective provincial governments were providing subsidization for both non-profit and for-profit centers, found that non-profit status was associated with indicators of higher quality (Friesen, 1992; West, 1988). Therefore, it appears that something other than the availability of government funding is responsible for the differences in quality usually found between for-profit and non-profit centers. Friesen (1992), a sociologist, suggests that the differences in quality are related to differences in organizational structure and methods of operation between for-profit and non-profit programs. One example would be the difference in the average percentage of budget devoted to staff salaries and benefits between for-profit centers and non-profit centers that was discussed above.

❖ ❖ ❖ ❖ Summary

Contextual factors directly impact on certain aspects of the child's daily experience, the adult work environment, and the structural features of the program. These relationships are illustrated in Fig. 8.1 on page 107.

Figure 8.1

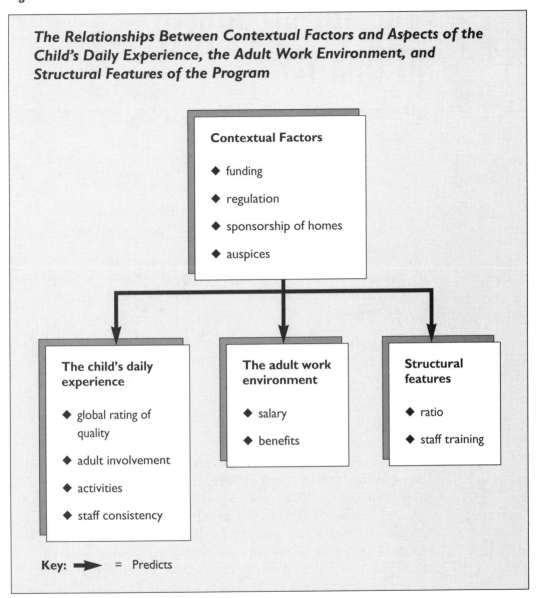

The Relationships Between Contextual Factors and Aspects of the Child's Daily Experience, the Adult Work Environment, and Structural Features of the Program

Contextual Factors

◆ funding

◆ regulation

◆ sponsorship of homes

◆ auspices

The child's daily experience

◆ global rating of quality

◆ adult involvement

◆ activities

◆ staff consistency

The adult work environment

◆ salary

◆ benefits

Structural features

◆ ratio

◆ staff training

Key: ➡ = Predicts

9 The Maintenance of Quality

The previous chapters examined the research findings related to:

◆ the interaction between the adult and the child and other important aspects of the *child's daily experience*, for example, staff consistency and programming;

◆ the *structural features* of early childhood programs, for example, provisions for health and safety, the staff-to-child ratio, and staff training;

◆ the *adult work environment*, for example, salary level and the administrative style of the program director; and

◆ *contextual factors*, for example, the level of funding and the strictness of the regulations in the jurisdiction in which the program operates.

Each of these can be thought of as a **category** of related items, for example, the category "child's daily experience". So far, the categories have been discussed in isolation from each other and as if there was a simple linear relationship between each category and quality, as in A predicts B. However, the situation in actual programs is more complex. As discussed below, there is an inter-relationship among categories. Because of this, it is unlikely that making changes to only one category would significantly change the level of quality in a program. For example, only increasing wages would probably not significantly improve the child's daily experience in a program that had a large number of children per adult and staff with little training.

Just as a number of categories go into *obtaining* quality, there are a number of mechanisms for *maintaining* quality. Again, this chapter will discuss each mechanism separately for ease of presentation. However, it is probable that a combination of mechanisms for maintaining quality is more effective than the use of a single mechanism.

The Inter-Relationship among Categories: Everything Matters

When a substantial number of research studies is reviewed, as has been done in the previous chapters, it becomes evident that:

◆ the level of quality in a program often results from a combination of categories. For example, Whitebook et al. (1990) found that programs with good staff-to-child ratios tended to also have well-trained staff, and to pay good salaries. Conversely, programs with too many children per adult also tended to have staff with little training and low salary levels. Thus, the level of quality found in the program resulted from a combination of structural factors (ratio and staff training) and characteristics of the adult work environment (wages); and

◆ some categories influence child well-being and development both directly and through their impact on another category. Regulation, which is part of the category "contextual factors", directly influences children's level of language development (Goelman & Pence, 1988). Regulation also has an impact on the category "child's daily experience", for example, the staff-to-child ratio predicts the extent to which children receive appropriate caregiving (Phillips et al., 1992). The extent to which children receive appropriate caregiving, in turn, predicts their well-being and development.

Figure 9.1, on page 111, uses the research findings discussed in previous chapters to illustrate these two points. It shows, for example, that the category "structural features", at the top left-hand corner of the figure, directly predicts child well-being and development and indirectly influences the child through its impact on the child's daily experience. The structural feature of staff training predicts the amount and type of interaction between the adult and child. The amount and type of interaction predicts social and language skill development. It should also be noted that, in turn, the category structural features is influenced by the category contextual factors. For example, the level of funding available to the program influences the number of staff that can be hired and, therefore, structural features such as the staff-to-child ratio and group size. Ultimately, all four categories determine the quality of the early childhood program.

Mechanisms to Maintain Quality

Previous chapters have indicated some mechanisms for *obtaining* quality, these include:

◆ adequate funding to enable hiring sufficient staff, who have appropriate education and receive appropriate salaries and benefits;

◆ government regulations for licensing that require the levels of staff education, staff-to-child ratios, and group sizes that have been shown by research to be associated with quality; and

◆ regular communication between parent and staff as a way of increasing the consistency of the child's experience.

According to Morgan (1979), mechanisms to *maintain* quality fall into three general categories:

◆ **regulatory methods**. These include state, provincial, or territorial government regulations, local zoning by-laws, and local building codes;

◆ **voluntary standards of professional practice**. These include accreditation, credentialing, self-review, and peer review; and

◆ **other non-regulatory methods**. These include public and user education, in-service staff training, parent involvement, peer support networks, and consultation from other professionals.

Figure 9.1

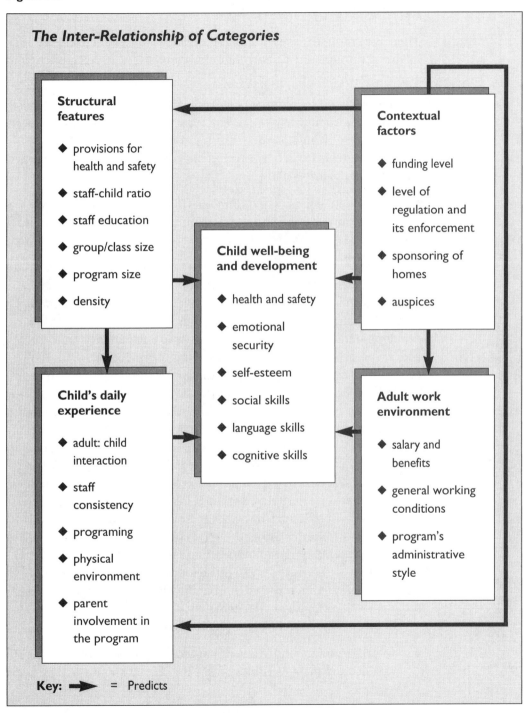

The Inter-Relationship of Categories

Structural features

- provisions for health and safety
- staff-child ratio
- staff education
- group/class size
- program size
- density

Contextual factors

- funding level
- level of regulation and its enforcement
- sponsoring of homes
- auspices

Child well-being and development

- health and safety
- emotional security
- self-esteem
- social skills
- language skills
- cognitive skills

Child's daily experience

- adult: child interaction
- staff consistency
- programing
- physical environment
- parent involvement in the program

Adult work environment

- salary and benefits
- general working conditions
- program's administrative style

Key: ➡ = Predicts

Regulatory methods

There is a common assumption that quality is most effectively achieved through setting and enforcing standards through government regulation. However:

◆ the legislated requirements represent the *minimum* that the society in question will tolerate. The extent of the relationship between quality and regulation depends upon the extent to which the requirements for licensing extend beyond the threshold of practice that might harm a child; and

◆ government licensing requirements in early childhood programs usually only address structural features, such as the staff-to-child ratio, even though the interaction between the adults and children is more important for quality.

In spite of the above, government regulation is valuable. Although structural dimensions cannot ensure that optimal patterns of interaction will occur between staff and children, or that programming will be developmentally appropriate, they appear to facilitate desirable interaction and programming. As discussed in the previous chapter, Phillips et al. (1992) found a statistically significant relationship between the level of the regulatory requirements in the state where the program was operating and the likelihood of children receiving appropriate caregiving and developmentally appropriate activities. Secondly, a number of research studies in both the United States and Canada have found that children from families at environmental risk are more likely to be enrolled in low quality early childhood programs than are other children (Anderson et al., 1981; Goelman & Pence, 1988; Holloway & Reichhart-Erikson, 1988; Howes, 1988; Howes & Olenick, 1986; Howes & Stewart, 1987; Kontos & Fiene, 1987; Schliecker et al., 1991; Vandell et al., 1988; White, 1989). Regulatory requirements for levels of structural features that are consistent with those found to be desirable by the research literature increase the probability that *all* children in licensed programs will receive a quality experience.

To be effective, regulatory standards must:

◆ be clearly and unambiguously worded, so that both the service provider and the government licensing official know exactly what is required;

- deal with features that are known to effect children's well-being and development;

- be observable, measurable, and enforceable; and

- be actually enforced. This means programs must be monitored, so that there is pressure to adhere to the standards, and sanctions must be applied for non-compliance. In North America, sanctions for non-compliance most often take the form of issuing a provisional or temporary license, with a time limit by which the non-compliance must be addressed. A license is usually only withdrawn or denied if the non-compliance puts children at risk.

Effective regulation also requires support for the legislated standards. For example, if staff members are required to have a certain level and type of education, this education must be accessible and affordable.

Voluntary standards of professional practice

Morgan (1979) identifies accreditation, credentialing, self-review, and peer review as the most common forms of voluntary standards. She refers to them as "voluntary" because they are not mandated by a governmental authority.

Accreditation

Accreditation is a process by which a representative body, recognized by both the service community and the community in general, establishes standards for services. These standards are above the minimum regulatory standards set by government. Programs apply on a voluntary basis for evaluation against the standards and, if found to meet or surpass them, are granted a certificate that recognizes this fact. Accreditation is considered valuable because it articulates a community's agreed upon indicators of quality, provides a goal to aim towards, and recognizes those programs that are providing quality services. The process, which involves self-evaluation followed by a comparison done by trained outside observers, is, in itself, considered educational for the program and its staff. In the United States, the National Association for the Education of Young Children has a national accreditation system for early childhood programs. In Canada, other services, such as hospitals, can go through an accreditation process but there is, as yet, no national accreditation program for child care or other early childhood programs.

Credentialing

Credentialing enables experienced staff, who have little or no formal education related to the provision of child care, to demonstrate that they have equivalent skills to those of people with a diploma or certificate in early childhood education and/or to obtain these skills. In the United States, the federal government established a Child Development Associate (CDA) Program in 1972. This has identified specific skills and knowledge considered to be desirable for people working in an early childhood program. Experienced staff can voluntarily register to be evaluated by a team of professionals who observe the person in their current work situation. As a result of this observation, the person may be deemed "competent" and granted a Child Development Associate credential, or may be identified as requiring training in certain areas of practice. In the latter situation, the person can obtain the suggested training and then reapply for credentialing. For additional information on the Child Development Associate Program, see Perry (1990) and Powell & Dunn (1990). Increases in child development knowledge and positive adult behaviors have been found after participation in Child Development Associate Program training by Peters & Sutton (1984) and by Saltz & Boesen (1985).

In Canada, Manitoba has provided a credentialing opportunity for people already working in child care, but lacking formal early childhood education, since the mid-1980s. Manitoba uses a procedure modeled after the American Child Development Associate Program process, but modified to conform to provincial requirements. In 1992, an evaluation was conducted on 60 people who had received a certificate of competency under this program. The study included interviews with the 60 people, the person who had functioned as their advisor during the time they sought credentialing, the center supervisor or director where the person did their supervised experience, and the supervisor or director of the center where the person currently worked. The study found that 90 percent of the people still worked at the center where they had done their supervised experience, and that all 60 people obtained high ratings as child care providers by the supervisor or director of their current workplace (Cooper, 1994).

Self-review

In self review, a program examines itself to identify whether it needs to make changes. To be effective, this approach requires the use of an objective process, and the implementation of a plan to address any changes identified as being required. Kontos & Stevens (1985) tested the *Early Childhood Environment Rating Scale* (Harms & Clifford, 1980) in child care centers in the United States to determine its usefulness as a self-review tool. They report that the centers found it easy to use, and that the specificity of the scales helped people to pinpoint exactly what needed to be changed. This scale, and its related scales for other age groups, are widely used by Canadian programs for self-review. California requires all state subsidized child care programs, home-based as well as center-based, to conduct a yearly self-review using an instrument designed by the State. Programs are expected to be able to document that they have done the self-review within the past year, have developed a plan to address areas of weakness identified by the self-review, and have actually implemented the plan (California State Department of Education, 1988). These requirements underline the importance of acting on the findings of a self-review.

The National Association for the Education of Young Children (1983) has pointed out the need for programs to conduct an annual evaluation of the performance of each individual staff member. The Association suggests that this evaluation be based on classroom observation, using predetermined criteria that have been shared with all staff members in advance of the evaluation.

Peer review

In peer review, a person or group of people from another early childhood setting do an on-site visit to review the program. Usually this is done through the use of a standard measurement tool, such as the *Early Childhood Environment Rating Scale* (Harms & Clifford, 1980).

The people doing the evaluation then discuss their findings with the program's staff. The advantage of a peer review is its greater objectivity relative to self-review. At the same time, it preserves the value of having the review conducted by people who are actively engaged in providing a similar service. Both the program being reviewed, and the people doing the review, can learn from each other.

Other non-regulatory methods

Other non-regulatory methods for encouraging and maintaining quality include: public and user education, in-service training for staff, parent involvement, peer support networks, and consultation from other professionals.

Public and user education

Morgan (1980) suggests that both public and user education are necessary to:

◆ raise community expectations for the level of staff education, and for the type of programming in early childhood programs; and

◆ support government efforts to improve quality. For example, if the general public understands the importance of staff-to-child ratios, public support for government financial assistance to early childhood programs is more likely. As discussed in the previous chapter, financial assistance, over and above funds raised through parent fees, increases a program's ability to have appropriate staff-to-child ratios.

Members of the public tend to believe that government licensing is an assurance of quality. Few people seem to realize that government officials are only able to make a limited number of visits to a program in any given year. In contrast, particularly in child care, parents usually drop-off and pick-up their children on a daily basis. They are the people, other than staff members, who are in the best position to monitor what is going on in a program. However, parents can only monitor effectively if they understand what quality is and know how to determine whether or not it is present. User and parent education can be done through a variety of means, for example, through television programs, or through pamphlets distributed through physicians' offices or available in local supermarkets.

In-service training

The research leaves no doubt about the relationship between formal education in child development or early childhood education and quality in early childhood programs. However, the acquisition of knowledge should not stop when the person completes his or her formal education. Research by Black et al. (1981), Goodman & Andrews (1981), Jones & Meisels (1987), Kaplan & Conn (1984), and Whitebook et al. (1990) demonstrates the value of in-service education for both center-based and home-based caregivers.

Parent involvement

Chapter 5 discussed the value of ongoing communication between the parent and the program staff. Not only does this increase the likelihood of greater consistency between home and program for the child, but also an informed parent can monitor what is going on and express concern about practices that may not be conducive to quality. Both American and Canadian experts have suggested that parents can have a positive impact on the quality of their child's program by either participating in a parent advisory committee, or by being a member of the program's board of directors. Some North American jurisdictions require licensed child care centers to have either a parent advisory committee or user-parents on the board of directors. Unfortunately, there appears to be no research that has specifically tested the hypothesis that parents in this type of decision-making capacity actually impact on the quality of the program.

California requires all preschool child care programs receiving state funds to involve parents in an annual written evaluation of the program (California State Department of Education, 1988). Winget et al. (1982), in Minnesota, sent questionnaires to all the parents using, or who had recently used, one of 950 home-based child care programs. Over 500 questionnaires were returned. Each completed questionnaire was shared with the relevant caregiver. Licensing officials reported that the parent feedback was helpful in identifying deficiencies in the homes that they had not picked up, and also in enabling them to reinforce desirable caregiver behavior.

Peer support networks

The formation of local peer support networks by centers or home-based child care providers offers opportunities to share information, for peer consultation or review, for joint staff training, and for moral support. As discussed earlier, home-based child care providers who are sponsored, and therefore part of a peer network, obtain higher ratings on a global measure of quality (Pepper & Stuart, 1992) and engage in larger amounts of behavior likely to facilitate child development (Carew, 1979; Fosburg, 1981).

Consultation from other professionals

Consultation from other professionals provides the opportunity for a different perspective, as well as a different body of knowledge, to be applied to the program. As will be discussed in Chapter 11, consultation from other professionals, such as physiotherapists, is essential for the provision of a quality program for children with special needs.

10 Celebrating and Supporting Cultural Diversity

We live in a society characterized by a wide range of people of various appearances, abilities, racial backgrounds, ethnicity, languages, and religions. The original inhabitants of North America belonged to many distinct nations with different **cultures**, that is, different languages, religious practices, ways of looking at the world, and ways of behaving. The Cree, the Navajo, and the Ojibway were and are as distinct from one another as are the peoples from different European nations. In the 1600s, settlers began to arrive in North America from various parts of Europe. More recently immigrants have come from all over the world. Anyone living in North America who is not a descendant of one of the original inhabitants is an immigrant or the descendant of immigrants. Thus, cultural and racial **diversity** (differences) are not new and will continue to be a fact of life. Furthermore, immigrant children and **visible minority** children (children of African, Asian, or Native ancestry) born in North America live in both urban and rural areas. Cultural diversity, therefore, is not simply a characteristic of big cities.

The Rationale for a Multicultural Approach

Multicultural early childhood programming acknowledges, understands, respects, and supports diversity and actively rejects prejudice or bias in regard to race, ethnicity, cultural background, religion, or language. Children's appreciation of cultural diversity is not best fostered in early childhood programs by providing children with isolated experiences, such as a meal of Mexican or Vietnamese food. Rather, this appreciation is best produced by providing children with daily experiences that emphasize and value the fact that people in our society come from different backgrounds. There are a number of reasons for using a multicultural approach, including:

◆ the ongoing reality of living in a multicultural society;

◆ children's early awareness of cultural and racial diversity; and

◆ the fact that ethnic and cultural identity are an integral part of the child's self-concept.

The ongoing reality of a multicultural society

Because we live in a multicultural society, even children who are born into a homogeneous neighborhood are unlikely to live all their lives in a similarly homogeneous community. Inevitably, almost any child living in North America will be in a situation at one time or another where others have different beliefs and different ways of behaving. Therefore, it is important for children to develop the attitudes and skills required to live and work comfortably with people from various backgrounds. This is best done during the early childhood years when children can learn to view differences in appearance and ways of doing things as interesting and positive rather than as distressing or threatening.

Children's early awareness of cultural and racial diversity

Between age two and three, children begin to show a clear awareness of physical differences such as skin color and hair texture. This is hardly surprising. Learning colors occurs when the child is two and children of this age are encouraged to notice differences. As early as age three, children may begin showing signs of **pre-prejudice**, that is, discomfort with people who are different from them and their family members. For example, a child may be reluctant to hold the hand of a darker-skinned playmate. Research indicates that by age four or five, many children are developing definite attitudes towards people from other racial backgrounds or cultures. An American study of 100 Black and White children aged three to five found that 25 percent of the sample expressed strong race-related values by age four (Derman-Sparks et al., 1990). By the age of six, children have developed the basis of the attitudes and values which will stay with them for the remainder of their lives (Mock, 1982).

It is inaccurate to assume that young children are unaffected by the prejudices and biases of the larger society. Parents of children attending multicultural child care centers in Canada reported that name calling, such as "Dumb Paki", was prevalent in the programs attended by children as young as age three. The parents also reported that their children were hurt and bewildered by such comments (Mock, 1989).

Growth of the child's self-concept

Children learn to act, believe, and feel in ways that are consistent with those of the significant adults in their lives. These are usually family members. Therefore, the child learns the **culture** of his or her family. Its way of viewing the world, language patterns, concepts of acceptable behavior, attitudes, and learning styles are transmitted at an unconscious level through repeated adult demonstration and comment. Different countries have different cultures which in turn have different definitions of what is normal human behavior. For example, the cultures of Italy and Greece encourage open and spontaneous displays of emotion through voice, body gestures, and facial expressions. Chinese-based cultures tend to value emotional restraint and self-control as a sign of maturity and expect it from even very young children. The culture-bound beliefs, feelings, and accepted ways of behaving that the child learns at an early age contribute significantly to the child's definition of self (**the child's self-concept**).

By age four or five, children have a well-developed concept of their own racial identity. Derman-Sparks et al. (1990), in a report from a study of children's comments about race, give examples of a White four-year old asking why she is White while her friend is Black and a four-year old coloring with a brown crayon and saying to himself, "I'm brown too." Immigrant or minority children of this age, or younger, are also aware that they are Polish, or Mexican, or Cherokee.

Children who, as a result of experiences such as name calling, come to feel that their race or culture or ethnic group is inferior cannot develop a strong sense of self-esteem. Confidence in oneself is necessary for making friends and for the risk-taking required for learning. Children who do not learn quickly may be discriminated against by teachers. This can lead to further development of low self-esteem. Cummins (1986) notes that there is considerable research linking school success with the extent to which minority children's language and culture are incorporated into the school program. Early childhood programs can encourage and support the child's identity and the development of a positive self-concept by incorporating materials and activities that respect and affirm the child's race or ethnicity, by addressing signs of bias or discrimination, and by promoting collaboration between the program and the home.

◆ ◆ ◆ ◆ Implications for Practice

Very few studies have been conducted to examine what is required in an early childhood program to assist children from all backgrounds to develop a positive self-concept and the attitudes and skills needed to live successfully in a multicultural society. Therefore, unlike the previous and following chapters, the discussion of desirable practice in this chapter is based primarily on informed opinion rather than on research findings.

High quality programs recognize individual differences in the children and build on the child's past experiences (one aspect of **developmentally appropriate practice**). However, it is easy to fail to recognize the cultural biases that ignore individual experience in many North American early childhood programs. These biases include materials, toys, activities, and foods that are based solely or primarily on the North American White middle-class experience. In a multicultural society, some young children may be more familiar with tortillas than with bread and some children come from a family where children are encouraged to make choices while other families believe the child should wait to be told what to do. In order to provide a high quality program, the cultural and ethnic background of each child must be taken into consideration and the program adjusted accordingly. It is also important to recognize that families differ within the same ethnic or cultural group and not all members of a culture have exactly the same childrearing practices (Kilbride, 1990).

People sometimes express concern that acknowledging or pointing out the differences that occur in a multicultural society will encourage prejudice. However, children do notice differences at an early age. This, in itself, is not the problem, nor is the problem the differences themselves — the problem lies in how people respond to differences. Denying a child's awareness of differences, for example, responding to a child's question about another child's dark skin with, "We are all the same under the skin," does not help children to make sense of their experience. Failing to confront children's misconceptions or discriminatory behaviors encourages lack of tolerance and has a negative impact on the self-esteem of the child who faces discrimination.

Interaction between adults and children

Children learn from the behavior and comments of others, especially significant adults in their lives. The interaction between the adult and child may reinforce or teach bias without deliberate intent or may encourage self-acceptance and acceptance of diversity. Children sometimes react to cultural or physical differences with discomfort and harmful words or behaviors. Whether this is simply a response to newness or difference, or a learned prejudice, the adult must intervene. Contact with other children from different cultural, racial, or ethnic backgrounds does not seem to be sufficient for children to develop positive attitudes towards and to feel comfortable with diversity.

John said to his teacher, "Ana talks funny." Calmly but firmly his teacher responded , "Ana does not talk funny. Ana is from Brazil where they speak Portuguese. Ana speaks very good Portuguese, now she is learning English. In our class we help children to learn English."

If the teacher had responded, "Ana is from Brazil, she can't help how she talks," she would have implied agreement with John that somehow Ana was inferior. Her actual response pointed out that Ana could speak another language well, implied acceptance of the way Ana speaks English, and provided John with the guidance that he was expected to help Ana. It is also important to be on guard for one's own unintended discriminatory remarks. Telling a group of children, "Quiet down, you are acting like a bunch of wild Red Indians," implies a negative view of Native peoples.

The following guidelines for interaction between adults and children in a multicultural situation have been suggested by Derman-Sparks and the A.B.C. Task Force (1989) and by Kilbride (1990):

◆ do not ignore either questions about diversity or discriminatory behavior;

◆ intervene immediately;

◆ try to understand what the child is really asking or means so that you can act appropriately. Is the child's question a seeking of reassurance that they are alright even if they are Black? Is what appears to be discriminatory behavior in a child who has not previously shown such behavior simply a problem of two children wanting the same toy at the same time?

◆ give an explanation that is appropriate for the child's developmental level. A three-year-old asking about another child's skin color needs only to be told it is because that child's parents have that skin color. The child does not need a lesson on the biological basis of skin color;

◆ set limits, for example, clearly state that it is not fair to exclude someone because of who they are and that such behavior is not tolerated in your class; and

◆ comfort and support the targets of discriminatory behavior and provide them with assurance that they are alright.

These guidelines are illustrated by the following examples:

> *During lunch Pavarti, a two-and-a-half-year-old of East Indian descent, asked why she was brown. Sonia replied "Each of us has a different and special color. You are a beautiful brown like your mother." Then Sonia went around the table pointing out Sean's pink skin and red hair, Jenny's tan skin, brown eyes, and black hair, and so on. Every so often she referred to another skin or hair color as being beautiful or lovely.*

Sonia's matter-of-fact response acknowledged Pavarti's observation of being different. Her use of the phrase "beautiful brown", and her pointing out that the other children differed from each other, supported Pavarti in gaining a positive self-concept. If Sonia had abruptly said, "Oh, it doesn't matter what color you are, I like you all," her response could have conveyed the message that she liked Pavarti in spite of the fact she is brown.

> *In the playground, five-year-old Eric pulled his eyes up at the corners and yelled out to Kiyoshi, "Hey, slanty eyes, slanty eyes." Mr. Balut, who was passing by, stopped and asked, "Eric, why are you making fun of Kiyoshi? You will hurt his feelings." Eric responded defensively, "His eyes are funny." Mr. Balut replied, "His eyes are not funny. They are a different shape from your eyes because his parents' eyes are a different shape. Kiyoshi has the same shape eyes as his parents, just as your eyes are the same shape as your mother's and father's. Both shape of eyes are equally good for seeing with. It's O.K. to ask questions about why people look different, but it is not O.K. to say they look funny or to call them names." Mr. Balut then turned to Kiyoshi and said, "I'm sorry that Eric made fun of your eyes. You have brown eyes, I have blue eyes, they are both equally good."*

Mr. Balut did not ignore name-calling even though he was not responsible for Eric's classroom. His pointing out that eyes of different shapes are equally good for seeing with helped to focus Eric on what is important about eyes. His statement that it is not alright to call people names gave a clear message that he would not tolerate prejudice.

> *Jeff, Krystyna, and Luis were making a house with craft materials. Jay came over wanting to join in but Krystyna pushed him away saying, "Go away. Indians aren't allowed." Jay turned and started to walk away. Lori, having overheard the remark, went over to Jay, put her arm around him, and gently turned him to face the three children. She then said, "Being Apache is no reason for not being able to do something. It is not fair to tell Jay he cannot join you in making a house because he is Indian." Before she could continue, Krystyna interrupted with, "Indians are bad." To try to understand the reasoning being used by Krystyna, Lori asked, "Why do you feel that way?" Krystyna responded, " Indians kill people and burn their houses. I saw them do it on TV." Lori then told her, "Krystyna, some programs on the TV about Indians and White settlers are make-believe. Sometimes Indians did fight the settlers, but this was when they were defending their families. In our room everyone plays with everyone else. Now, how can Jay help you with the house you are making?"*

Lori used the concept of fairness and unfairness, an idea that children grasp at an early age, to give a clear message that what Krystyna did was unacceptable. Then she explored why Krystyna had behaved that way and tried to correct her misconceptions based on the TV program. Finally, Lori reaffirmed every child's right to participate in all activities by asking how Jay could help the others.

The physical environment

As noted by Chud & Fahlman (1985, page 84):

> deliberate or not, what is included or excluded in the classroom environment speaks plainly about what is valued by educational institutions and by teachers. If a program's physical setting includes only images and materials from one

culture, then the validity, importance and equality of unrepresented cultures is diminished in the eyes of those children and families.

Chud & Fahlman suggest that priority be given to the specific cultures of the children enrolled in the program. However, if staff and children in the group are all of one culture, then the staff should create an environment which is representative of the multicultural nature of the larger community. In an all-Black classroom, this would mean creating an environment which also reflects White culture. Strategies for developing an appropriate setting include:

◆ the use of pictures, which may be cut out from magazines, that show people from various cultures engaged in *ordinary* life experiences, such as grocery shopping. It is important not to depict people from other cultures only doing special activities such as a once-a-year religious celebration;

◆ the provision of dolls, toys, books, and puzzles that reflect a diversity of racial and cultural groups. In this way, all the children can be sure of being able to identify with some of them and all the children are exposed to new experiences;

◆ avoidance of materials that contain stereotypes, for example, a set of "cowboys and Indians" figures; and

◆ props for pretend cooking and work activities and clothes for dress-up that reflect different cultures.

Having only one picture or one doll that depicts another culture is not sufficient. The aim is to blend items from various cultures so that the children experience cultural and racial diversity as an everyday occurrence.

Programming

Derman-Sparks and the A.B.C. Task Force (1989) provide the following guidelines:

◆ connect cultural activities to concrete daily life. Young children cannot relate to abstract concepts;

◆ explore cultural diversity within the principle that *everyone* has a culture. White families have different ways of doing things just as people of different races do;

◆ have cultural diversity permeate the daily life of the classroom through frequent, concrete, hands-on experiences related to the children's interests;

◆ begin with the cultural diversity among the children and staff; and

◆ avoid assumptions or statements about homogeneity, for example, remarks such as "Jamaicans eat ackee, rice, and salt cod."

In a multicultural setting, children and staff can be encouraged to share aspects of their life so that racial, ethnic, or cultural differences are related to people the children know. Children may be asked to bring in a picture of their whole family and then discuss with each other how their different families do things. This could include roles of various family members inside and outside the home, for example, grandmother looks after me when Mom is at work, the foods that are eaten regularly, recreational activities, and special holidays. It is best to focus on what the adults do, rather than where they work, since some parents may be unemployed. By using the children's families as a basis for a discussion of diversity it is easier to avoid stereotypes. Instead of, "All Japanese eat sushi which is made of raw fish," the teacher can elaborate on Kiyoshi's information that he eats raw fish at home by observing, "Some of the raw fish dishes Kiyoshi's family eat are called sushi. " A variation of this activity is to have staff and children bring in items from home for identification and discussion. These should include things from White homes in recognition that White people also come from different cultures. If staff or children speak different languages, the class might be taught how to sing "Happy Birthday" or its equivalent in each language. Support for an open acknowledgment and discussion of differences comes from research that has found that children's understanding and acceptance of diversity increased in programs where cultural similarities and differences were openly and positively acknowledged in daily routines and activities (Chud & Fahlman, 1984).

Holiday celebrations from another country can be a fun way to reinforce the concept of diversity as positive. Children can help prepare and then share a special meal, make decorations, and learn the appropriate songs. However, if holidays are the main focus of a multicultural curriculum it will fail to give the children a sense of everyday life in other cultures. The celebration of special days can be supplemented by listening to cassettes from different cultures, learning songs in different languages, using instruments such as an African drum or an East Indian sitar, and playing games from other countries. Snacks may include matzos and pita bread or mangoes. Children may need to be taught how to react to unfamiliar food, that it is alright to say, "I have never had something like this." It is not alright to say, "Ooh, yucky," since that might hurt someone's feelings. During circle time, books can be read which reflect ethnic or racial diversity. The books used should be about children from various cultures engaged in familiar activities such as going shopping with mother or the first day at school. Diversity can also be supported by providing art materials that include various skin-tone crayons, play dough in a spectrum of shades from tan to light to dark brown, and paints in colors such as tan, light brown, and dark brown as well as pink so that children can select a color close to their skin color.

In a situation where all the children and staff are from one ethnic or racial group, the adults will have to initiate discussion about diversity and set up opportunities to talk about similarities and differences. A first step can be taken by helping children to explore differences among the group. When children are playing beside a full-length mirror, the adult can ask them questions about their skin, hair, and eye color. Even in an all-White situation children can see differences in skin shades, including freckles. The technique of having children bring in a picture of their whole family and describe it can also be used since family traditions and food preferences will differ. **Persona dolls** might also be used. These are dolls that accurately reflect a given culture, are given an appropriate name and history which is shared with the children, and then used to tell stories about everyday activities in the doll's family. Another strategy is to invite guests who are members of various cultural and racial groups to visit the program. However, Kendall (1983) cautions that the guest be introduced on the basis of what they have to offer, for example, "Mrs. Wong is going to tell us about her job as a police officer," not, "Today we have a Chinese lady visiting us."

Family involvement

In a program serving primarily White children

In a program composed primarily or exclusively of North American-born White children, some parents may not see any reason for a multi-cultural approach. It may help them to understand the need if you point out that experience with and understanding of different cultures is part of the necessary preparation for life in a multicultural society. In a situation where there is a mixture of ethnic groups, there may be some mutual distrust of each other among parents. Kendall (1983) and Ramsey (1987) suggest that in these situations it may be helpful to bring parents together informally, for example, at a pot-luck supper, so they can talk about their children and observe the similarities in their hopes for their sons and daughters.

The importance of involving the family

A wide variety of behavior can constitute normal childrearing practices within a given culture. Childrearing practices may be even more varied across cultures. Yoshida & Davies (1982) found that Canadian-born parents use different discipline methods and have different expectations than East Indian parents living in Canada. Similarly, childrearing practices differ between East Indian parents living in Canada and Canadian residents born in the Caribbean. If boys are excused from helping in household tasks at home, but are expected to participate in clean-up in their early childhood program, or if exploration is valued in the program, but at home the child is expected to wait for adult direction, the different expectations can cause confusion and anxiety for the child. This, in turn, has a detrimental effect on the development of the child's self-confidence, and self-help and social skills. Diversity based on ethnicity, race, or religion can be a source of inconsistency of expectations between program and home. Therefore, it is important in a program with children from various backgrounds for staff and parents (or another family member who has major responsibility for rearing the child, such as a grandmother) to share childrearing approaches, to discuss major differences in expectations, and to try to reach a compromise. If a compromise in approach cannot be reached, the early childhood program staff can clarify for the child that at home Mom and your sisters do the tidying but here we all help, both ways are fine. Such a response shows respect for the family's approach and reduces the confusion for the child. The adult's acceptance of childrearing differences also demonstrates acceptance of and respect for diversity.

> *"I'm not Black," Jesse, a dark-skinned Black preschooler insisted during a discussion on skin color. His teacher, worried about his self-concept, tried talking to him later on an individual basis. He still insisted, "I'm not Black." When Dad picked Jesse up that afternoon, the teacher told him about the incident. The father laughed and said, "I know what is happening, we use the term Afro-American." The next day when the teacher referred to Jesse as an Afro-American, he repeated, "I'm Afro-American," with great pride.*

The above incident highlights the importance of finding out from parents what terms they use to describe themselves and what they have taught their children about their ethnic and racial identify. A special example of this need occurs in the situation of children whose parents come from two racial backgrounds or children who have been adopted into a family of a different race.

Lee (1989) points out the importance of ensuring the availability of interpreters if there is no staff member who speaks the parent's language so that the parent and program can exchange information and ideas. Even when language difference is not an issue, it is necessary to remember that interaction style is influenced by culture. For example, some cultures require a person to look down when speaking to someone in authority; this may be interpreted by a person raised in North America as being evasive rather than as a sign of respect.

It is also important not to confuse cultures, for example, to assume that all Native Americans or all Latinos have the same childrearing practices and traditions. Again, parents, grandparents, and other significant adults in the child's life can provide assistance. Band elders have been found to be a particularly valuable resource in teaching language, spiritual beliefs, traditions, music, and stories in both an Inuit program in northern Canada (Canning, 1986) and in a Native American program in New Mexico (Hilgendorf, 1984).

Final Observations

Various cultures, races, and ethnic groups are only one aspect of diversity in our society. There is gender diversity, diversity in physical ability, and diversity in intellectual ability. The multicultural approach discussed in this chapter focuses on diversity arising from different physical appearances, different ways of looking at the world, different beliefs and traditions, and different languages. The following chapter looks at quality early childhood programs for children whose diversity results from different physical or intellectual abilities. A common theme in both chapters is assisting children to feel comfortable with themselves, to feel comfortable with others' differences, and to interact with others in a non-biased way. The same applies to gender differences. This general approach to diversity of gender, ability, culture, ethnicity, and race is called **anti-bias programming (or curriculum)**.

This chapter and the following chapter also re-visit themes raised earlier in the context of identifying what makes a quality program. These themes include:

◆ treating each child as a unique individual;

◆ being responsive with and encouraging of the child and providing ample opportunities for two-way communication;

◆ engaging in developmentally appropriate practice;

◆ involving parents in a meaningful way on a continuing basis; and

◆ providing children with a variety of stimulating opportunities for exploring their world.

11 Quality Programming for Children with Special Needs

A child is considered to have special needs whenever he or she requires help and information beyond what is normally required by a child of the same age in order to assure the best developmental outcome (Canning & Lyon, 1990). The additional assistance may be required because the child has a physical disability that limits motor activity, or a developmental delay or handicap, such as Down Syndrome, that results in intellectual limitations. Other reasons for requiring additional help or information are: visual and/or hearing impairments, communication problems, a chronic medical condition such as kidney disease, behavior problems, or being at environmental risk.

As noted in Chapter 1, there is a substantial body of research that demonstrates the ability of high quality early childhood programs to compensate for the home environment of a child at environmental risk. The behavior of staff in such programs, and the characteristics of the programs themselves, for example, staff-to-child ratio, are the same as those described as being desirable in Chapters 3, 5, and 6. Therefore, this chapter will not discuss programming for children at environmental risk.

Wolery et al. (1992) note that young children with special needs are tremendously diverse, for example:

◆ within a given condition, such as hearing impairment, the impact on the child's development may be mild, moderate, or severe depending on the extent of the disability and the extent to which mechanical assistance, such as a hearing aid, can compensate for the disability;

◆ two children with the same diagnosis, for example, cerebral palsy, may have very different developmental levels; and

◆ disabilities can occur in isolation or in combination. One child may have a communication difficulty while another may have both a communication difficulty and behavior problems.

Because children with special needs are children, they have the needs shared by all children for safety, physical care, emotional security, and opportunities for skill development. However, they also have needs not shared by other children. These include the need for:

◆ professionals who can assess the child's individual strengths and weaknesses and use these in the development of intervention plans to encourage the child's development; and

◆ early childhood program staff who can work cooperatively with people from other disciplines, such as speech and language therapy.

In some situations, modifications to the physical environment are required to assist the child's skill development and to minimize the impact of the child's disability on the child's ability to be independent.

◆ ◆ ◆ ◆ The Rationale for Mainstreaming

The inclusion of children with special needs into ordinary programs along with other children who do not have special needs is now preferred practice. This approach is called **mainstreaming** or **integration**. The rationale for mainstreaming is based on:

◆ civil rights;

- the expectation that the development of the child with a special need will be as good as or better than what would occur in a **segregated** program, that is, a program where all the children have special needs; and

- the expectation that children without special needs will benefit from ongoing involvement with children who have disabilities.

The civil rights argument

Segregation by race, disability, or other personal characteristic is wrong because it excludes the individual from participation in normal community life. Children with special needs have a right to education and care in their own community and on-going contact with children who live in their immediate neighborhood. Segregated programming often requires the child to be transported to another community for service, thereby reducing contact with neighbors. Segregation also labels the individual. Labeling is undesirable because it stresses perceived deficiencies and, by emphasizing group membership, minimizes perception of the child as an individual.

Gains for the child with special needs

An assumption is made that mainstreaming children with special needs will benefit them because:

- the children who do not have special needs will **model** (demonstrate) age-appropriate behaviors for the children with special needs and these children will imitate such behaviors;

- the mainstreamed setting will provide a more advanced **linguistic** (that is, language), social, and cognitive environment than would be provided in a segregated program. This will "push" children with special needs to acquire more advanced skills (Odom & McEvoy, 1988); and

- children with disabilities who are in a mainstreamed program will learn to be comfortable with non-disabled peers (Striefel et al., 1991).

Gains for the child who does not have special needs

It is as necessary to help children to gain the attitudes and skills to live and work comfortably with people who have disabilities as it is to prepare them for life in a multicultural society. Mainstreaming is advocated as a way to help children without disabilities to understand disabilities and to learn to respect differences in others (Irwin, 1993).

Research Findings

Researchers have examined:

◆ the impact of enrollment in a mainstreamed program on children age zero to six who have or do not have special needs; and

◆ the effectiveness of different programming strategies with children with special needs who are in a mainstreamed early childhood setting.

The impact of mainstreaming on children

There are three main issues, as outlined below.

◆ Do children with special needs gain from being in a mainstreamed program?

◆ Does mainstreaming have any negative impact on children without special needs who attend such programs?

◆ Do children without special needs gain from being in a mainstreamed program?

The impact of mainstreaming on children with special needs

Social interaction is the direct exchange of words, gestures, toys, or other materials between two or more children. A primary goal of mainstreaming is the provision of an opportunity for children with special needs to participate in activities and develop positive social relationships with other children. The assumption is that social interaction will provide opportunities for **modeling** (demonstration) of age-appropriate behaviors by the children without special needs and, as a result, the social, communication, and cognitive skills of the child with special needs will improve.

All the studies that have examined social interaction have involved children with developmental disabilities or autism. This raises the question of whether the findings are also applicable to children whose special needs arise from other conditions. Odom & McEvoy (1988), in a review of 18 studies that examined patterns of social interaction in mainstreamed early childhood programs, concluded that:

◆ left to their own devices, normally developing children tend to interact more frequently with other non-disabled children or with children who have only a mild disability than with peers who have a moderate or severe disability. Similarly, children with moderate or severe disabilities tend to interact more with other children who have disabilities than with non-disabled children; and

◆ social interaction will probably not occur between children with moderate or severe disabilities and non-disabled children unless it is specifically fostered by the program staff.

Using a peer rating scale, Strain (1984) examined the friendship patterns of children in mainstreamed preschool programs. He found that acceptance or rejection of children with a developmental disability was related to the extent to which the child with the disability had been engaged in positive social interaction with the non-disabled peer. This study underlines the importance of encouraging social interaction as a step towards increasing the likelihood that friendships will occur between normally developing children and children with disabilities.

Odom & McEvoy (1988) reviewed 10 studies that examined the

developmental gains made in communication and social skills by preschool children with special needs in mainstreamed programs. It should be noted that most of these studies did not compare the gains made by the mainstreamed children with the gains made by a comparison group of children enrolled in segregated programs. Therefore, they cannot answer the question of whether children with special needs make greater developmental gains in mainstreamed or in segregated programs. Furthermore, while some studies included children who were deaf or blind, none included children with behavior problems or special needs resulting from a chronic medical condition.

On the basis of the studies they reviewed, Odom & McEvoy concluded that:

◆ generally, although not always, the mainstreamed children with special needs made gains in social and communication skills that could not be attributed to **maturation** (increased age) alone; and

◆ children with special needs made greater developmental gains in situations where there was specific programming to stimulate skill development.

The impact of mainstreaming on *the cognitive skills* of children with developmental delays, such as Down Syndrome, appears to have been evaluated by only one study. This involved 80 children aged three to six with a variety of developmental delays who were in either segregated or mainstreamed programs in 14 different American communities. No significant difference was found in the rate of cognitive skill development between the group of children in mainstreamed programs and the group in segregated programs (Fewell & Oelwein, 1990).

Odom & McEvoy caution that it is difficult to draw conclusions from a small number of studies. Nevertheless, they suggest that simply putting children with special needs in the same classroom as peers who do not have special needs is not sufficient to stimulate skill development. Their view is supported by research that indicates that the developmental progress of individual children depends more:

◆ on the quality and type of program than on integration alone (Cooke et al., 1981; Fewell & Oelwein, 1990; Jenkins et al., 1989; Strain, 1990); and

◆ on appropriate staff training (Guralnick, 1982; Hanline, 1985; Smith & Greenberg, 1981).

The impact of mainstreaming on children without special needs

It is as important to ensure that children without special needs are not harmed by mainstreaming as it is to determine whether children with special needs make gains in mainstreamed programs. Odom & McEvoy (1988) reviewed five studies that examined the impact of mainstreaming on the non-disabled children enrolled in such early childhood programs. Again, none of the programs studied included children with behavior problems or special needs resulting from a chronic medical condition. Four of the studies found that the non-disabled children made the gains that would be expected on the basis of maturation in either language and/or cognitive skills. The fifth study found that non-disabled children made greater gains in non-mainstreamed programs. Again, this is a small sample of studies that used a variety of different measures. However, the studies suggest that participation in a mainstreamed early childhood program probably has no negative impact on the development of children without special needs.

One rationale for mainstreaming is that it will assist children without disabilities to understand and be comfortable with people who have disabilities. Stoneman (1993) notes that little research has been conducted to explore the validity of this assumption. The few studies that have been done indicate that:

◆ by age three, children are definitely aware of physical disability and understand that it imposes limitations on motor abilities. They tend to assume that the physical disability imposes other limitations not associated with motor ability, for example, intellectual limitations; and

◆ children age three to six prefer to interact with children who do not have a disability even when they understand that the child with the disability has the ability to participate in the activity in question.

Stoneman suggests that these findings indicate that mere contact with children who have disabilities is insufficient to increase non-disabled children's understanding of disabilities and their degree of comfort interacting with people who have disabilities.

Research on programming strategies

Developing social skills

Many children with special needs, including those with physical and/or communication disabilities, lack age-appropriate social inter-action skills (Guralnick & Groom, 1988; Odom & Brown, 1993; Wolery et al., 1992). As a result, other children are reluctant to involve them in their activities. From their review of the research, Odom & Brown (1993) suggest that the following strategies are effective in developing social interaction skills among children with special needs who are enrolled in mainstreamed early childhood settings:

- **incidental teaching.** The adult, during unstructured activities such as free play, provides the child with a visual or verbal cue (**a prompt**) to join other children in an activity, to imitate the behavior of a more socially competent child, or to use social skills learned during specific individual training sessions. If the desired behavior results, it is then **reinforced,** that is, followed by praise, a tangible reward such as a happy face sticker or some other means of encouragement;

- teaching the children who do not have special needs to support the social interaction of the children with special needs through initiating interaction with them, showing them how to do something, and/or providing reinforcement for the child's social interaction efforts. This approach often requires the teacher to provide both prompts and reinforcement for the children without special needs in order to encourage them to interact as desired with the children who have special needs; and

- a combination of training by the adult and the use of children without special needs. For example, training both target and other children in specific social skills then using prompts and reinforcement for both groups to encourage the use of the skill in daily activities.

The research indicates that removing children with special needs from the general group to give them specific skill training is effective in teaching social skills. Unfortunately, the skills learned do not appear to

transfer from the setting in which they were learned to the general early childhood program or the child's home. In other words, the skills are only shown by the child in the training setting.

Developing language skills

Research indicates that direct instruction by the adult through the use of demonstration, prompting, and reinforcement is effective in teaching language and communication skills to children with special needs. However, children seem unable to transfer what is learned in the direct instruction sessions to other settings (Notari & Cole, 1993). Warren & Kaiser (1988), in an extensive review of studies involving incidental teaching of language skills to children with special needs in a mainstreamed early childhood setting, found that this approach appears to be successful. Skills learned also transfer across settings, for example, into the child's home. Training normally developing peers to initiate and maintain communication with children who have language problems has also been found to be an effective strategy (Goldstein et al., 1988; Jenkins et al., 1989).

◆ ◆ ◆ ◆ Implications for Practice from the Research

Summary of the research findings

The research findings discussed above indicate that:

◆ social interaction will probably not occur between children without special needs and children with moderate or severe disabilities unless it is specifically fostered by program staff — simply putting the two groups of children together is insufficient;

◆ children with special needs can successfully be taught skills through the use of training sessions that remove them from the general group. However, the skills learned in such training sessions are not likely to transfer to other settings;

- children with special needs are more likely to make developmental gains if the mainstreamed program specifically stimulates their skill development;

- children with special needs are more likely to make developmental gains in mainstreamed programs where the staff have received specific training; and

- mere daily contact with children who have disabilities is insufficient to overcome the misconceptions of children without disabilities or to increase their degree of willingness to interact with people who are disabled.

Staff training

Each child with a special need is unique. While all children with Down Syndrome have some characteristics in common, each has individual ways of behaving, likes and dislikes, and life experiences. The principles of responsiveness and developmentally appropriate practice require that each child be treated as an individual, not as a category with a certain type of disability. As noted in Chapter 3, staff training directly predicts the quality of the child's experience and, through this, the child's well-being and development. Therefore, all adults working directly with children in an early childhood program should have had training in child development and early childhood programming for normally developing children. In addition, in order to provide a quality experience for children with special needs, the adults must:

- know the causes and characteristic manifestations of the specific disabilities of the children being served;

- be familiar with what is known about the usual development of children who have these disabilities;

- be aware of specific strategies that have been found to be necessary or useful with children who have these disabilities;

- have had specific training related to assessing and meeting the individual child's needs, for example, how to position *this* child in her wheelchair; and

◆ on-going skill maintenance training, for example, to ensure that the staff member is still using the correct technique for changing a bladder catheter.

The early childhood program staff also need to learn how to make the most effective use of consultation from disciplines such as physical, occupational, and language therapy. The **transdisciplinary approach**, that is, people from different disciplines working together in order to assist the child, is discussed in a later section of this chapter.

Involvement of the other children

By the age of three, children are definitely aware of physical disabilities. However, their limited experience and understanding often means that they think they can "catch" a disability simply by being involved with a disabled person. They also tend to assume that physical disability imposes other limitations, for example, that a child in a wheelchair is also less intelligent than non-disabled age-mates (Derman-Sparks and the A.B.C. Task Force, 1989; Wolery et al., 1992). Given the above, it is not surprising that the research has found that putting young children with special needs in the same program as children without special needs is not sufficient to ensure social interaction between the two groups. Adult encouragement is required. Experts also suggest that before a child with a disability enters a program, the other children in the program be provided with basic information about the child's specific disability (Striefel et al., 1991).

> *Four-year-old Rachel, who was new to the class, stared at Ricardo from a distance but was obviously reluctant to go near him. Joe, who was working with the group, squatted down beside Rachel, pointed to Ricardo and the children with him, and said encouragingly, "Come and paint with Ricardo and the others." Rachel looked at Joe with wide eyes and responded, "Don't want to." "Why?" Joe asked. "Cuz," said Rachel. Joe looked at her and asked, "Are you afraid of Ricardo?" Rachel nodded yes. Joe then asked "What do you think will happen if you play with Ricardo?" "Don't know," whispered Rachel.* ➡

> *Understanding that Rachel may never have seen a person in a wheelchair, and perhaps thought she would "catch" Ricardo's disability, Joe explained, "Ricardo has to use a wheelchair because his legs don't work. When people need a wheelchair it is because of something that happened before they got the chair. Playing with Ricardo won't hurt your legs — the other children have been playing with him since September and they can still walk." Joe then took Rachel by the hand and walked her over to where Ricardo and the other children were painting.*

The staff person can also arrange situations that will encourage children without special needs to interact with children who have disabilities and to learn that a disability in one area does not automatically mean limitations in other areas. If eight children want to be in the dramatic play area at one time, but there is only room for four, the children and teacher can set up a schedule so that one group plays there for the first 30 minutes and then the second group gets a 30-minute turn. The teacher can arrange the groups so that each includes some of the children with special needs. Or a child with a disability who knows many shape and color names can be paired with a child without special needs whose ability is not as advanced. During a classification game, the child with a disability can teach the other child and, in spite of the disability, is put in a situation of having an advantage in relation to the other child. This type of experience helps the child with special needs to develop a positive self-concept and shows the other children that different people have different skills and abilities.

As noted above, the research has found that children without special needs can assist children with special needs to develop social and communication skills. A description of the procedures used is beyond the scope of this chapter (see Odom & Brown, 1993 and Warren & Kaiser, 1988). However, the general observation can be made that staff need to be on guard for non-disabled children being over-protective of children with special needs.

> *Savita, who has a hand prothesis, was learning to feed herself. She was still having difficulties, even with a specially modified spoon. May, another child, began feeding Savita who accepted this arrangement. The teacher intervened, saying, "May, I'm pleased you want to help Savita; however, this is not a good way. Savita is learning to feed herself and needs to keep trying." She then turned to Savita and told her, "Savita, you can do it. Remember how well you did yesterday? Show me how you can use the spoon yourself."*

Programming

The research has found that developmental gains are more likely to be made if the child with a disability receives specific programming. Furthermore, gains are more likely to be made if the skills are learned and practiced in the general group setting. The Division for Early Childhood of the Council for Exceptional Children in the United States recommends the development of an individual educational program (IEP) for each child through the collaboration of the child's family, the early childhood program staff, and other relevant disciplines. Wolery et al. (1992) note that at a minimum, each IEP should include: a summary of the child's current level of functioning, annual goals, short-term objectives, identification of special services required, dates of initiation and expected duration of special services, and identification of the specific individuals responsible for implementing the IEP and their individual roles.

◆ ◆ ◆ ◆ Other Implications for Practice

Wolery et al. (1992) note that quality early childhood programs for children with special needs require:

◆ on-going involvement of the child's family in a way that respects the family's values and priorities;

- the involvement of people from a variety of other disciplines, for example, an occupational therapist; and

- appropriate modification of the physical environment.

Family involvement

Quality early childhood programs, as defined in Chapter 1, support and complement the family in its childrearing role. This acknowledges the central role of the family in the development of young children. When the child has a special need, consistency of approach between the home and the early childhood setting assists the child's skill development and reinforces the approaches being used in each of the two settings. The principles of good practice advocated by both the United States' Division for Early Childhood of the Council for Exceptional Children (1993) and the United States' National Association for the Education of Young Children (Bredekamp & Rosegrant, 1992) emphasize the importance of involving the family in setting goals and developing programs for children with special needs.

To collaborate effectively with families in determining their needs and their goals for their child, and to involve them in planning appropriate programs, the early childhood program staff must:

- be sensitive to cultural diversity; and

- avoid preconceived ideas of family roles, behaviors, and goals.

In some cultures, a relative other than the parent, for example, a grandmother, may have primary responsibility for the child in the home. This family member must be included in any collaborative effort between home and early childhood setting. It is important to be aware of the different perspectives on disability among different cultural groups. These can have a direct impact on how you go about establishing a collaborative relationship with the child's family. As noted by Hanson (1990), some cultures view disability as fate and as something that has to be endured. Other cultures recognize disability as something that may simply happen and do not take the position that nothing can be done to improve the situation. Similarly, in some cultures the child's disability is viewed as the result of something the mother did wrong in pregnancy, or as punishment for a sin; therefore, it is the family's fault and the family's total responsibility. Such families find it difficult to accept, let alone seek, assistance from non-family members.

The transdisciplinary approach

No single profession prepares its members to adequately assist all children who have special needs and their families. Few mainstreamed early childhood settings are able to employ the range of professional disciplines needed to address the variety of special needs that may be exhibited by children in the program. The need for input from and involvement by different disciplines in order to provide developmentally appropriate programming for children with special needs and to encourage their development can by obtained through **consultation**. This approach involves a specialist, such as an occupational therapist or a nurse, assisting the person engaged in the direct service provision to provide a more appropriate and effective service to a person with special needs. For example, a psychologist may assist a junior kindergarten teacher to identify and implement strategies to reduce a child's aggression instead of the psychologist seeing the child in individual therapy sessions. Not only does this approach increase the amount of "therapy" the child receives, it also provides the teacher with knowledge and skills that may be useful with other children.

Much of the research conducted to examine the effectiveness of the consultation approach has been conducted in elementary or secondary schools. This raises the question of whether the findings apply to early childhood settings. File & Kontos (1992) suggest that the common aspects of the consultation process across settings make it appropriate to assume that the positive child outcomes demonstrated in other settings would occur in programs for children under age six. Research suggests that the most effective form of consultation is a **collaborative** model which assumes that the specialist and the person receiving the consultation both have unique knowledge and skill to contribute to joint problem solving and intervention planning.

The **early childhood resource teacher** model is also used in several North American jurisdictions (Frankel & McKay, 1990). Ideally, the individual has basic training in early childhood education, for example a two-year community college diploma, plus additional formal post-secondary school training related to children with special needs. The early childhood resource teacher may work solely at a specific center or provide assistance to a number of centers on a rotating basis. The individual may conduct assessments, provide direct service to individual children or a small group of children with similar needs, provide consultation to other staff working in the program, do home visits and provide home management training and/or parent counseling, provide liaison between services used by the child and the early childhood program, and/or conduct staff training workshops. When the model was first developed it usually involved the resource teacher working directly with three or four children with special needs as a separate group within a mainstreamed program. As noted by Irwin (1993), removing the child from the general program for activities in a special group or therapy in a clinic has the following disadvantages:

◆ it reduces the amount of contact other staff have with the child and thereby their awareness of the child's learning style and the special techniques that are effective with that child;

◆ skills learned in the separate group or at the clinic may not **generalize** (that is, transfer) to the general early childhood program;

◆ removal of the child for part of the time isolates the child from sharing, turn-taking, and waiting, which are natural elements of the group experience and skills that the child needs to acquire; and

◆ the child misses out on some opportunities to learn from other children.

Frankel (1994) observes that increasingly the early childhood resource teacher model is moving towards a collaborative consultation approach to assist the program staff to incorporate activities as part of the general program, and moving away from direct service delivery to children.

Hanson & Widerstrom (1993) note that other disciplines can also be effectively used to:

◆ provide on-site workshops designed to provide information about disabilities in general and to foster information exchange on issues related to providing services to children with special needs;

- provide on-site training in the specific skills required for a particular child; and

- provide information about resources.

Some children, particularly those under age two, may be participating in a part-time specialized program as well as attending a mainstreamed early childhood program. The consistency of approach that is so important for child skill development makes it essential that staff from the two programs meet on a regular basis and jointly plan the interventions to be used with the child.

The physical environment

The requirements for the physical environment for any high quality early childhood program outlined in Chapter 5 also apply to a mainstreamed setting. In addition, if there are children with limited mobility, building modifications such as ramps, grab bars, and doorways sufficiently wide to accommodate a wheelchair may be required to foster children's maximum independence. Care is also needed to ensure that toys, books, and materials can be reached by a child in a wheelchair or walker or who is using crutches.

For the development of a positive self-concept, children with disabilities need to see themselves reflected in the environment. This may be accomplished by having pictures showing people with various disabilities engaged in ordinary daily activities, bought or home-made dolls wearing a brace, with thick glasses or other obvious evidence of a disability, and books about people with disabilities. Pictures, toys, and books need to include males and females and to reflect various ethnic backgrounds as well as disabilities.

Final Observations

The Division for Early Childhood of the Council for Exceptional Children in the United States has published a manual outlining indicators of quality for early childhood programs serving children with special needs (1993). As noted by McLean & Odom (1993), there is great similarity between the practices recommended in this publication and those recommended by the National Association for the Education of Young Children (Bredekamp & Rosegrant, 1992) for normally developing children. This Association's recommendations are, in turn, similar to those indicated by the research findings discussed in this book. The recommendations of the two organizations differ in that the Division of Early Childhood puts greater emphasis than does the Association for the Education of Young Children on:

◆ the concept of developmentally appropriate practice including the concept of being appropriate for the child's chronological age. This means treating the child with a disability the same as any other child of that age to the extent that his or her abilities permit. For example, it is not age-appropriate to carry a three-year-old who is able to use a wheelchair independently. If the program is not on the ground floor, there should be an elevator so that the child can get to the program independently just as the child's peers do by using the stairs; and

◆ a transdisciplinary approach to programming.

The above two points represent differences in emphasis, not differences in recommendations. The consistency in recommendations between an organization representing young children in general and one representing children with special needs is noteworthy. It indicates that good practice applies to all children.

12 Research Methods

Until recently, recommended practice for early childhood programs was largely based on theory and the informed opinion of practitioners with many years of experience in the field. Reviews of the existing research have concluded that there is sufficient consistency in the findings to reliably identify many of the components of early childhood programs that are associated with child well-being and development (for an example of research reviews, see Hayes et al., 1990; Phillips & Howes, 1987). As a result, we can confidently say we *know* what is required, not merely that we *think* that such-and-such is necessary for quality in early childhood programs.

◆ ◆ ◆ ◆ Different Methods

Several methods are used to study the impact on children of adult behaviors in, and the characteristics of, early childhood programs. These include:

◆ laboratory experiments;

◆ observations in the early childhood program and/or home;

◆ administration of standard tests to measure development level; and

◆ interviews or questionnaires.

Each method has strengths and weaknesses, and none is more "scientific" than another. The meaningfulness of the method depends on the question being asked. Some questions are best approached using one method, others are best approached using another method. In many instances, a combination of methods provides the most information.

The laboratory experiment

The laboratory experiment is modeled after methods used in the physical sciences, for example, biology and chemistry. This method allows the researcher:

◆ to control conditions so as to rule out all influences on behavior except the influence being studied; and

◆ to compare two groups of subjects who are matched on a number of characteristics deemed to be significant because they could impact on the outcome, for example, children's age and length of experience in an early childhood education program.

Suppose you wanted to determine whether young infants have a preference for pictures of human faces over other visual stimuli, for example, a picture of an animal or a checkered pattern. In a laboratory experiment you could present different visual stimuli in a quiet room where there were no other visual stimuli that might distract the infants. You could determine what appears to interest the infants most by noting precisely the amount of time spent looking directly at each picture, or perhaps even record the children's brain waves as each visual display is presented. In contrast, if you conducted the same experiment in the infants' homes you would have to contend with background noise and other distractions which might reduce the children's attention on the pictures you were presenting. Control and precision are the chief advantages of a laboratory experiment.

Some studies examining the outcome of early childhood programs with different characteristics, or classified as having different levels of quality, have used laboratory experiments. The following description of a laboratory experiment to determine the impact of high quality early childhood programs in contrast to low quality early childhood programs comes from a study conducted by Howes & Olenick (1986). Their study actually used a combination of methods, therefore the following is only a partial description of their methodology.

> *Several early childhood programs were classified as high or low quality on the basis of the combination of the staff-to-child ratio, level of staff training, and staff turnover rates. Children were selected from four "high quality" and four "low quality" programs to participate in the study. The subject selection was done so that there was no significant difference in the group of children from the high quality programs and the low quality programs in age, number of boys and girls, membership in a one- or two-parent family, father's occupation level (for example, blue collar, white collar or professional), parents' ethnic background, or parents' educational level. The child and his or her parent participated in a 30-minute laboratory session. During this time, each parent-child combination was asked to complete the same two tasks, one involved a boring activity and the other was to clean-up. In addition, the children on their own were given two self-regulation tasks, one was not to touch an attractive toy and the other was not to eat a snack. Sitting behind a one-way mirror, so that she could see the children but they could not see her, a research assistant, who did not know whether the child in question was in high quality or low quality child care, observed and recorded what went on. Children from the high quality programs were found to be significantly more likely than the other children to complete the two tasks and significantly less likely to touch the forbidden toy or eat the snack.*

The important aspects of the methodology to note in this example are:

♦ the standard method used to classify programs as high or low quality;

♦ the care taken to ensure that the two groups of children were similar to each other in characteristics that might influence their behavior, such as age. This was done to rule out as much as possible all influences on the children's behavior other than the influence being studied, namely, program quality;

♦ the fact that precisely the same tasks were given to all the children; and

♦ the fact that data collection was done by a research assistant who did not know whether the child being observed was from a program classified as high or low quality. This is important to eliminate any bias that might result if the observer knew which type of program was being attended by a child being observed.

While laboratory experiments have the advantages of permitting control and precision, they also have certain disadvantages. For one thing, their results do not always apply to real-life situations. Children may behave differently in an unfamiliar laboratory setting than they would in their own home or in an early childhood program they had been attending for several months. Secondly, many questions of interest are not suitable for study in an experimental situation. For example, a researcher would not want to deliberately expose children to harsh and restrictive caregivers in order to study the impact of the adult's behavior on children's development. However, the impact of adult harshness and restrictiveness on children is an important research issue. The researcher can, however, study this issue by observing children in early childhood programs where they are already being exposed to harsh and restrictive adults. This approach is called **naturalistic observation**.

Naturalistic observation

In this approach, behavior is observed in everyday settings as it occurs naturally. Researchers go into homes, early childhood programs, and playgrounds to watch and observe the everyday behavior of adults and children. When doing this, the researchers are precise and systematic in recording what they see. For example, they develop a standard observable definition for the behavior (or behaviors) they want to examine. They may also count how often the behavior (or each type of behavior) occurs, note how long each incident of behavior lasts, and/or note the sequences in which behaviors occur. Researchers do not simply watch what is going on and try to remember, instead they record as the behavior occurs. The following description of research using naturalistic observation comes from a study conducted by Vandell & Powers (1983).

Child care centers were classified as high or low quality on the basis of the combination of staff-to-child ratio, whether or not all staff had post-secondary school training in early childhood education, and the extent to which there was a good variety and number of toys available for the children. Children were selected to participate in the study in such a way that there was no significant difference between the children from the "high quality" and the "low quality" programs in terms of average age, belonging to an intact two-parent family, and average length of prior attendance in child care. Definitions of observable behavior were developed for a number of behaviors, including: child solitary behavior, child unoccupied behavior, child positive behavior with adults, child positive behavior with peers, and child negative behavior with peers. Before the study began, the people who were going to do the observations practiced observing and recording the behaviors until each person's observations agreed with another person's observation of the same situation 98 percent of the time or better. This gave an inter-rater reliability of 98 percent. In the study, each child was observed in the center for 16 minutes during unstructured free-play periods over the course of one day. The child's behavior was observed for 20 seconds, then immediately recorded before the next observation was made. The people doing the observation did not know whether the program in question had been classified as high or low quality. The children from high quality centers were found to have significantly fewer incidents of solitary or unoccupied behaviors or negative behaviors with peers. They also exhibited more incidents of positive behavior with adults and peers.

The important aspects of the methodology to note in this example, in addition to the aspects also found in the previous example, are:

◆ the development of specific definitions of observable behaviors to be used by each observer and with each subject:

◆ the development of high inter-rater reliability using the definitions that would be used in the study before the study began. As a result, it is possible to be confident that each observer was coding a specific activity engaged in by a child in the same way, that is, using the same label; and

◆ the use of an approach that involved observing for 20 seconds and then immediately recording the observation before the person had an opportunity to forget what the child was doing.

Naturalistic observation has the advantage of describing human behavior in real-life situations and has become the method most frequently used in early childhood program research. However, without some structure applied to this method it is difficult to explain what is observed. For example, suppose you visited a number of centers and observed that in some centers the children seemed to be more involved with each other while in other centers they more often seemed to be engaged in solitary or unoccupied behavior. You might wonder if the reason for the difference in child behavior reflected differences in the quality of the programs. However, you would have no way of knowing if this was the case simply on the basis of your observations. Some centers may have had a large number of new children and their solitary or unoccupied behavior might have reflected the children's lack of familiarity with the setting. In the example given above, the researchers used a standard approach to classify centers, ensured that the children were similar on important variables that might have influenced their behavior, and used standard definitions for behaviors. Therefore, we can feel confident that the observed differences in behaviors resulted from the differences in the extent to which the centers had trained staff, who were each responsible for a reasonable number of children, and who were in a situation where there was a good variety of toys. Because of the subject selection process used, it is highly unlikely that the differences in observed behavior resulted from differences in the family characteristics of the children or their having different lengths of experience in child care.

Administration of standard tests

Suppose you wanted to determine if a specific adult behavior encouraged children's language development. You might do this by developing an observable description of the adult behavior, then observing adults in a number of early childhood settings and administering a standard test of language development to all the children in the programs. To ensure that any differences in the scores obtained by children on the language tests reflected the impact of the specific adult behavior, you would want to ensure that the children were similar to each other in characteristics that might influence their level of language development, for example, child age. Similarly, you would want to ensure that the programs were similar in major characteristics, for example, the staff-to-child ratio. If all the children in programs where the specific adult behavior occurred frequently received higher scores on the test of language development, you would have reason to assume that the adult behavior made a difference.

The administration of standard tests, such as the *Peabody Picture Vocabulary Test* (Dunn, 1979), is attractive to researchers because it provides a measurement tool that has already been developed and tested in other situations. However, many standard tests used in North America to measure children's skill levels are based on an assumed experience that is North American, White, and middle-class. As a result, children from another culture (who, for example, may be unfamiliar with some of the objects pictured in the *Peabody*), or from a non-White or a socially disadvantaged home, may do poorly on the test. In this situation, the children's poor performance is a result of the test used and may have nothing to do with the aspect of the early childhood program that was being studied.

Interviews and questionnaires

Whitebook et al. (1990), in the United States, used standard interviews with 1,209 child care center staff members to obtain information on their work environment and to identify links between aspects of the work environment and the frequency with which people left their job (staff turnover rate). Using a standard list of interview questions has the advantage of ensuring that the same information is collected from each subject. In addition, the interview method allows for clarification of questions by the person being interviewed and clarification of responses by the researcher. Disadvantages of the interview method include the fact that it is very time-consuming. Secondly, interviews usually have to be conducted at a pre-arranged time so that the researcher keeps on schedule. This may be very inconvenient for the person being interviewed if, at the time scheduled, some crisis is occuring in the program.

A nation-wide study conducted in Canada surveyed 969 child care centers and 2,887 staff members through a mail-out questionnaire (Canadian Child Care Federation/Canadian Child Care Advocacy Association, 1992). On the basis of the data collected, the researchers were able to confirm the link between poor salaries and job dissatisfaction found by Whitebook et al. (1990) and to produce a detailed profile of the characteristics of people who work in child care centers in Canada. Questionnaires have the advantage of permitting the researcher to collect standard data from a very large number of people in a short period of time. In addition, the person providing the data can, within reason, choose to complete the questionnaire at a time that is convenient for them. In contrast, when being interviewed, people are under some obligation to make themselves available at the arranged time regardless of what else may be happening in their lives.

However, mail-out questionnaires also have disadvantages. First of all, the questions must be very carefully worded so that the person responding understands what is meant. Researchers try to increase the likelihood that this will be the case by conducting a **pilot test**. This involves using the questionnaire (or list of interview questions if this is the approach to be used) on a practice basis with a sample of people similar to the people who will be surveyed. Their responses are examined to determine if apparent confusions exist. The people may also be asked to identify questions they found confusing. Then, if necessary, the questionnaire is modified. Researchers also often provide the name of a contact person and a telephone number on the questionnaire so that if a recipient is unsure what a question means, he or she can seek clarification. A second disadvantage is that the return rate for mail-out questionnaires is often very low. It is not uncommon to have only a third of the questionnaires that were mailed out returned, even when a self-addressed and stamped envelope is provided.

A combination of methods

Researchers in early childhood education often use a combination of methods. When Howes (1990) wanted to determine the impact on children's social adjustment in kindergarten of each of: being enrolled in child care before age one, the quality of the child care setting, and the quality of the interaction between child and parent, she used:

◆ naturalistic observations of the children in both their child care programs and their homes;

◆ observation of each child and parent in a laboratory experiment;

◆ interviews with parents regarding family life; and

◆ completion of standard questionnaires by teachers to determine various aspects of the child's social competence.

The use of a combination of methods provides a richness of data not possible with only one method.

Different Timeframes

Concurrent research

Concurrent studies examine the impact of the early childhood program on the child while he or she is still in the program. Usually data is collected on only one occasion or over the space of only a few days. The advantage of this method is that the study can be completed quickly. However, it provides only a snapshot at one point in time. Longitudinal studies enable the determination of the long-term impact of the factor being studied, for example, the early childhood program.

Longitudinal research

Longitudinal studies follow the same group of individuals over a number of weeks, months, or even years. Suppose you wanted to know the impact on a child's peer social skills in kindergarten of having been enrolled in full-time child care before the age of one. You could select a group of infants who had entered child care before age 12 months and another group of infants whose parents planned to raise them entirely at home until they entered kindergarten. To increase the likelihood that any differences found did, in fact, reflect the influence of having been in child care, you would select families as similar as possible in terms of socioeconomic status, marital status and satisfaction, general attitudes towards childrearing, and so on. Periodically, for example, every six months, you would assess the children's social skills. Each assessment would allow you to determine how the two groups developed. A final assessment might be done at the end of kindergarten.

Longitudinal studies provide data that is more useful for policy development and determination of good practice than that obtained from concurrent studies. However, they have disadvantages, one of which is the difficulty of maintaining the sample over the total period of time. Between observations some people move and may not leave a forwarding address, others decide they do not want to continue in the study. In some cases, the lost subjects may all belong to one group, for example, the group of children whose parents did not intend to enroll them in child care. As a result, the size of the two groups may no longer be the same or the size of one group may become very small. Problems associated with small sample size are discussed in the next section.

Common Methodological Difficulties

The study of early childhood programs is part of developmental psychology and shares many of its methodological concerns. As is true in developmental psychology, researchers looking at early childhood programs have problems with:

◆ sample representiveness;

◆ sample size; and

◆ controlling for irrelevant factors.

Sample representiveness

The extent to which research findings can be used to determine appropriate or desirable practice depends, to a large extent, on the **representiveness** of the sample used in the study. When research findings are used to develop policy, advocate for change, or suggest desirable practice, an assumption is being made that the subjects (for example, the children and the early childhood programs) are an accurate reflection of the larger population. In other words, that they are **representative** of it. In research related to early childhood programs, the issues pertaining to representiveness are:

◆ whether the study sample involves ordinary programs and children in general;

◆ whether the body of research includes studies involving children from different socioeconomic and cultural backgrounds; and

◆ whether the research findings apply to programs in the country in which people are using the findings to justify policy and/or practice.

The use of ordinary programs and children

Much of the early research that examined the impact of early childhood programs on children involved highly resourced programs that targeted children deemed to be at risk for developmental delays due to environmental factors. One example, which has been widely publicized because it exhibited long-term benefits, is the Perry Preschool Program (Berrueta-Clement et al., 1984). The children in this program exhibited significantly better social and intellectual functioning in elementary and high school than did age-mates from the same neighborhood who had not been in the program. However, the subjects were disadvantaged Black children from an American inner-city ghetto and the preschool program was specifically designed to compensate for a disadvantaged home environment. It was also operated under the direction of university child development experts. Therefore, the study represented neither children in general nor the usual range of early childhood programs available in an average community. As a result, it has limited usefulness in identifying principles of good practice for ordinary programs. In contrast, the studies cited in Chapters 3 through

8 of this book were all conducted in settings receiving the usual level of resources for their jurisdiction. Therefore, the programs were representative of the usual options available to parents in the community in question. In addition, none of the studies specifically targeted children from severely disadvantaged homes.

Including children from different backgrounds

Ooms & Herendeen (1989) express concern that many of the earlier studies that focused on ordinary community-based early childhood programs involved only White middle-class children. They feel that it is erroneous to assume that the findings that involved such populations would apply to children from a lower socioeconomic status or a non-White home. The need to include children from different backgrounds has been recognized by researchers. Recent studies have deliberately and successfully ensured a range of socioeconomic, racial, and ethnic backgrounds among the children in their samples (for example, Burts et al., 1992; Goelman & Pence, 1988; Howes, 1988; Kontos, 1991; Phillips et al., 1987; Schliecker et al., 1991; Whitebook et al., 1990). There is still valid reason for concern about the lack of studies including Native children.

Applying the research to a particular country

The majority of studies attempting to link specific components of early childhood programs with child outcome have been conducted in the United States. Some people have questioned whether American samples are representative of the population in Canada or other countries and whether American research findings are applicable outside the United States. During the past decade, a significant volume of Canadian research has been completed. Researchers in Canada have obtained findings consistent with those of their colleagues in countries as diverse as the United States, Bermuda, England, and Sweden. This suggests that:

◆ there is a common core of adult behaviors and program characteristics associated with positive child outcome for children in early childhood programs across these different countries; and

◆ it is appropriate to consider research from other countries when attempting to identify practices in early childhood programs that are likely to lead to positive outcomes for children within a given country. An exception would be if the research is from a country that clearly has a very different culture. While Bermuda, Canada, England, Sweden, and the United States are all different, their cultures are all based on the West European tradition.

Sample size

Some early studies involved fewer than ten settings and/or only a small number of children. This is a problem because unique characteristics of one or two members of a sample of ten exert a much greater influence on the findings than they would in a sample of 100. Thus, in a small sample, one or two settings can distort the findings. As the body of research on early childhood programs has grown, the findings of studies with small sample sizes have been collaborated by the findings of studies with larger samples. For example, the finding in several small studies that adults with post-secondary school training related to child development are more likely to exhibit behaviors known to encourage child development has been confirmed by Whitebook et al. (1990). Their study involved 1,309 center-based child care providers serving children ranging in age from infancy to age six. The consistency of findings across several studies increases our ability to feel confident that the findings are meaningful.

Controlling for irrelevant factors

As suggested in the discussion of the different research methods, it is important to control for influences on behavior other than the influence being studied. In research examining early childhood programs, failure to control for differences in the family characteristics of children in different programs can distort the research findings. This is of particular concern when children's scores on standard tests are being used to determine if a particular aspect of a program is associated with positive outcomes for children. Research in developmental psychology and early childhood education has shown that middle-class preschoolers obtain higher scores on tests of social skills (Moore et al., 1988) and on tests of cognitive functioning (Kontos & Fiene, 1986) than do children from a low socioeconomic background. Years of maternal education predict children's scores on intelligence tests (McCartney, 1984; Melhuish et al., 1990a, 1990b) and tests of language development (Goelman & Pence, 1987; McCartney et al., 1982; Schliecker et al., 1991). Therefore, comparing programs where most of the children are middle-class with programs where most of the children are not may result in findings of differences in the children's development that are at least partially the result of differences in family background.

Researchers have become aware of the need to address this methodological problem. They now either try to match the two groups of children being studied on relevant family factors or collect information on family background, such as socioeconomic status and parental education levels, and use a statistical procedure to remove its possible impact on the research findings.

◆ ◆ ◆ ◆ Implications for Practice

It seems reasonable to assume that if the report of a research study has been published in a professional journal, its methodology must have been appropriate. Therefore, the reported findings can be trusted. This, unfortunately, is not always the case. For example, studies are still published where it is clear that differences in family background among children were not addressed. Therefore, when we read research reports we must do so with a critical eye and a basic understanding of what is required for acceptable methodology.

A second issue is whether or not the findings are sufficiently meaningful that decisions can be based on them. The term statistically significant or significant refers to the extent to which a relationship between two items, for example, between adult behavior and child language development could have happened by chance. If a research report states that statistical analysis found a relationship was "significant at the .05 level", it means that the probability of this relationship having occurred by chance is less than 5 in 100. A significance at the .01 level means the probability is less than 1 in 100. Within the scientific community, significance at the .05 level is taken to indicate that the relationship is the result of the variable being studied, for example, that the adult behavior does impact on the child's language development. Therefore, the finding can be used for decision making, for example, to indicate desirable practice.

13 Emerging Issues

There are a number of emerging issues in the early childhood field that have a direct impact on the question of quality. These include:

◆ the concurrent enrollment of four- and five-year-olds in child care and kindergarten;

◆ mixed-age grouping in early childhood programs; and

◆ the interaction between the impact of the child's family and the impact of the early childhood program.

This chapter briefly describes each issue and suggests some implications for practice.

Concurrent Enrollment in Child Care and Kindergarten

At least three factors explain the increasing number of four- and five-year-olds who are concurrently enrolled in kindergarten and child care. The first is the increased number of women working outside the home and requiring care for their children while they work. The second is the perception of many parents that their children will get a head start in school readiness by being enrolled in a kindergarten program. Often, their expectation and hope is that the kindergarten will provide training in "academic" skills, such as counting and word recognition. The third is the increased availability of junior as well as senior kindergarten in some parts of North America. Kindergarten is free to the user while child care is not. It is often less expensive to use half-day junior and senior kindergarten programs, and supplement them with part-time child care, than to pay for full-day child care. Three concerns have emerged relating to children being enrolled in both kindergarten and child care at the same time. These concerns are the:

◆ fragmented situation when four- and five-year-olds whose parents work full-time experience two out-of-home group situations with two sets of non-parental adults and potentially two very different environments;

◆ different staff training and structural requirements between child care and kindergarten; and

◆ pressures on both kindergarten teachers and child care staff to provide formalized drills and instruction that is not developmentally appropriate for four- and five-year-olds.

Fragmentation of the child's experience

Betsalel-Presser et al. (1991), in a study of communication patterns and content between kindergarten teachers and child care staff involved with the same child in the same school building in nine different school boards in Canada, found that:

- only 30 percent of the 126 subjects said that they discussed difficulties encountered by the children with their counterpart in the other program that the child attended; and

- 85 percent stated they rarely, if ever, talked with their counterpart about the programming approach they used, current program activities, their expectations for children's behavior, how they motivated children in their program, or how they dealt with conflicts between children.

These are very troubling findings, especially since the study involved situations where the child care and kindergarten programs were in the same building.

As discussed earlier, consistency is important for young children in order to give them a sense of emotional security. Therefore, kindergarten and child care staff should know what children are permitted or not permitted to do, the type of activities being engaged in, and any significant events that occur in the child's life in the other's setting. This requires regular sharing of information. If it appears that there are significant differences between the two settings, the staff should discuss ways of making them more similar in regard to expectations of child behavior and programming approach.

The different requirements of child care and kindergarten settings

As discussed in earlier chapters, staff education, the staff-to-child ratio, and group size all influence the child's daily experience and the child's well-being and development. The research indicates that post-secondary school education in child development and early childhood education is probably the best preparation for center-based staff working with children under age six. Responsibility for an appropriate number of children, given their age, and a small group increases the likelihood of adult behaviors that encourage child development.

The education requirements for kindergarten teachers include a bachelor's level degree obtained from university, but there is no specification that this be in early childhood education. No North American jurisdiction requires child care center staff to have more than a two-year course in early childhood education. As a result of the current requirements, kindergarten teachers must have more years of formal education than child care staff, but their education does not have to be specific to children under age six. Child care staff in jurisdictions specifying educational level must have training in early childhood education, but it may be as little as one year of community college. In one situation, the type of education may not be appropriate. In the other, the length of education may be insufficient.

A study of child care centers in five different states strongly suggests that the staff-to-child ratio for children age 37 to 54 months should be 1:8 or less and the group size should be 18 or fewer (Howes et al., 1992). The United States' Academy of Early Childhood Programs (1984) and the Canadian Child Care Federation (1993) have both recommended a staff-to-child ratio of 1:8 to 1:9 for four- and five-year-olds, depending on the group size, and a group size of 16 to 18, depending on the staff-to-child ratio. Permitted group size and staff-to-child ratio is larger in both junior and senior kindergarten.

The result of the above differences in requirements is that the child's experience may be very different in the kindergarten program attended for part of the day and the child care setting attended for the remainder of the day. Since both kindergarten and child care serve children age four and five, it would seem appropriate to have an integrated approach to educating staff to work with this age group. The discrepancies in structural requirements suggest the need for the relevant departments or ministries in each state, province, or territory to adopt common standards pertaining to programs for four- and five-year-olds.

The issue of developmentally appropriate programming

Elkind (1987) observes, on the basis of research conducted over the past three decades, that young children learn differently from older children. Thus, the education of young children must be different from the education of older children. The education of young children needs to be in keeping with their unique modes of learning, and with their developmental tasks. Children between age three and six are in what

Piaget (1952) termed the **preoperational stage**. This is characterized by a concrete mode of thinking. They learn best by direct involvement with and manipulation of the environment, not through more abstract instruction. They are also in the period when the balance between a sense of initiative and a sense of guilt is struck (Erikson, 1963). What happens to the child in this age period influences the child's future willingness to explore and experiment rather than rely heavily on adult direction.

Children in kindergarten are more likely than those in child care to be exposed to formalized instruction intended to develop academic skills, and to be required to follow rules, sit still, and listen quietly to the teacher. One reason for this is the location of the program in a school setting. This exposes the kindergarten teacher to an environment that stresses the development of academic skills. Secondly, some parents deliberately enroll their children in kindergarten because they want them to be involved in academic readiness training and not just "playing around". Therefore, kindergarten teachers may experience considerable parent pressure to provide drills and formal instruction to improve academic readiness. Thirdly, some school districts require kindergarten programs to set goals, such as, "the student will be able to identify the lower case letters of the alphabet with 80 percent accuracy". Hatch & Freeman (1988), on the basis of interviews conducted in 12 school districts in Ohio, concluded that kindergartens are increasingly becoming paper and pencil oriented with workbooks, ditto sheets, and other formal instruction materials. Bredekamp (1987) has observed that when the kindergarten is academically oriented, the child care staff may feel pressured to introduce inappropriate academic instruction to help the children to "be ready" for kindergarten.

Experts, such as Elkind (1987) and Katz (1987), have identified the following risks associated with formalized instruction with four- and five-year-olds:

◆ stress as a result of the requirement to focus on a specific learning task being at variance with the child's natural mode of learning in the preoperational stage. The association between a developmentally inappropriate program of formalized instruction and stress among children in kindergarten has been demonstrated by Burts et al. (1992) and Love (1993);

♦ damage to the child's disposition to learn. The spontaneous learning of young children is self-directed. A child whose exploration is treated as a failure to attend may acquire a strong sense of guilt about any self-initiated activities and not learn the skills to be self-directive; and

♦ damage to the child's self-esteem. The focus on right and wrong answers inherent in formal instruction orients the child away from self-reinforcement and makes the child overly dependent on the adult as a source of self-worth. In addition, introduction of concepts and abstract thinking before the child is ready increases the possibility of failure and the child feeling stupid.

To strengthen the child's disposition to be curious, to explore, and to seek answers, opportunities must be provided for exploration, and this type of behavior must be encouraged.

♦ ♦ ♦ ♦ Mixed-Age Grouping in Early Childhood Programs

Most current education for people who are going to work in center-based child care or kindergarten programs assumes the division of children into narrow age groups. However, in small rural child care centers, it is not uncommon for there to be infants and toddlers, or toddlers and preschoolers, in one group (Doherty, 1994). Thus, a group may consist of children who range in age from two-and-a-half to six. In home-based child care, mixed-age groups are the norm. Over the past few years, there has been a growing advocacy for mixed-age grouping in early childhood programs both on the basis of theory, and on the basis of support from research findings (Katz, 1992; Katz et al., 1990; McClellan, 1993).

Theory

Increased out-of-home employment by parents has increased the use of early childhood programs. Because so many are structured into narrow age groupings, this has reduced the opportunity for the child to interact with children of other ages, whether they be siblings or neighborhood groupings. As a result, younger children lose opportunities to observe and imitate the greater social, linguistic, and cognitive competence of older children. Older children lose opportunities for the provision of leadership and assistance to younger children. Mixed-age grouping, by enabling children of different ages to interact on a regular basis, is believed to assist the social and cognitive development of all the children. In addition, the presence of different ages in the same group is thought to encourage developmentally appropriate practices by emphasizing individual differences and decreasing the probability of attempts to engage all the children in the same activity at the same time.

Observational studies have found that aggression is more likely to occur in same-age groups of children than in mixed-age groups (McClellan, 1993). Fighting may be reduced because there is a natural hierarchy in mixed-age groups. The younger children realize that they cannot successfully challenge the older children. At the same time, they can more comfortably yield to the dominance of an older child without the loss of face that might occur from submission to someone of the same age. It is also thought that caring about and for others is more likely to be learned if there are opportunities for such behavior. The mixed-age group provides the older child with daily situations where he or she can provide help to, or take responsibility for, younger children.

Experts believe that children whose knowledge level and cognitive skills are similar but not identical stimulate each other's thinking and cognitive growth. Vygotsky (1978) hypothesized a **zone of proximal growth**, that is, an area of cognitive competence within which the child cannot solve problems alone, but can in cooperation with a person of greater cognitive competence. The more experienced child can provide assistance by observing the less experienced child's behaviors, and then providing hints, guidance, or correction. The process is bi-directional. It is not simply a matter of the less experienced child synchronizing his or her actions and thinking with those of the more experienced child, a process that is undistinguishable from direct formal instruction. Rather, central to Vygotsky's thesis is the idea that, while two people start from different points, they arrive at a shared under-standing through a process of communication. In other words, the shared understanding is created during the course of the interaction.

Mixed-age grouping provides the older child with the opportunity to be the more experienced person with benefit both to that child, whose knowledge is reinforced in the process, and to the younger child, who develops a new skill.

Finally, as pointed out by Katz et al. (1990), mixed-age grouping acknowledges the reality that most young children are not equally mature in all areas of development at the same time. For example, a child may be more advanced in verbal reasoning than in peer social skills. In a mixed-age group, children can interact with younger children in areas where they lag, which is less stressful than having to interact with same-age children in those areas. At the same time, they have models of more mature development which they can imitate.

Research findings

McClellan (1991) compared teacher ratings of socially desirable behavior, friendship patterns, and aggression in 17 mixed-age preschool programs and 18 same-age programs. She controlled for family background, race, class size, and age through a statistical procedure. Teacher reports indicated that, in same-age programs, there were higher levels of aggression, and a larger proportion of children who were rejected or neglected by their peers, than in mixed-age programs. Other American research in preschool programs has found that younger children show more mature and complex play when relating to older children than they do when relating to same-age or younger children (Goldman, 1981; Howes & Farver, 1987; Rothstein-Fisch & Howes, 1988). They also make more use of verbal communication (Rothstein-Fisch & Howes, 1988).

It appears, however, that the age range in the mixed-age group may be a crucial factor affecting outcome. Sundell (1993) reports on research from Sweden involving 14 different child care programs. Four of the programs had children ranging in age from one to six years, four had children ranging in age from two to six years, four had children ranging in age between three and six years, and the remainder involved children with no more than one year's difference in age. In the programs with the *larger* age spans:

- there was a larger amount of mixed-age interaction among the children but fewer teacher-led activities; and

- the children had poorer language and cognitive skills than age-mates in programs where the age range was relatively small.

Sundell hypothesizes that a large age range makes it more difficult for the teacher to plan and execute teacher-led activities. As a result, the children are left more to their own devices than they would be in a situation where the children are closer in age. Another Swedish study found that mixed-age groups where the children were within 12 months of age were associated with higher social skills than those found in programs where the age range was greater (Sundell, 1993).

Implications for practice

Katz (1992) notes that simply putting children into mixed-age groups will not yield the potential benefits suggested by theory. The adult must provide a variety of activities where children of different ages can work together and each make their individual contribution to the joint effort. She also notes that, in a mixed-age group, there is the risk of younger children becoming overwhelmed by the competence of the older children or the older children perceiving the younger children as holding them back. Therefore, the adult must keep in mind the potential for overlooking the older children's need for challenge or pushing the younger children beyond their limits. The above requirements suggest a need for specific training for working with mixed-age groups.

Katz et al. (1990) raise the following questions about implementation of a mixed-age early childhood program.

1. What is the optimal age range?

2. What is the best proportion of younger children to older children?

3. What proportion of time should be spent in a mixed-age group?

4. What type of programming is appropriate?

They suggest that children too far apart in age will not interact sufficiently to benefit because the skills of the older child will be too advanced for the younger child to imitate. In their study of mixed-age groups in home-based child care, Rothstein-Fisch & Howes (1988) found that children aged 16 to 23 months used more imitation and verbal communication with two-year-olds than they did with preschoolers or infants. The researchers suggest that for the toddlers, the two-year-olds were sufficiently similar, yet sufficiently advanced, to create a zone of proximal development. In contrast, the preschoolers were too advanced to be appropriate and reciprocal peer partners. The Swedish research cited above suggests that an age range of one year is optimal for social skill development and a one- or two-year span facilitates language and cognitive development. The optimal age range may vary with the child's age, with, perhaps, preschoolers being able to benefit more from a larger age range than infants.

Katz et al. (1990) note there is no research on the best proportion of younger children to older children. They suggest that there must be a balance of ages that will prevent younger children from being over-whelmed and older children from regressing to the behavior of the younger children. Therefore, only two or three children of one age in a group of ten to twelve of another age is probably not desirable.

Again, there is no research that has examined what might be an appropriate proportion of time to spend in a mixed-age group. As pointed out by McClellan (1993), if the mixed-age group is large enough, it provides opportunities for interaction with both same-age and other-age peers. Therefore, the child can practice skills that are unique to same-age peers as well as those required with older or younger children. If, however, the group is small, for example, a home-based child care setting, it may be necessary to deliberately provide opportunities for same-age peer interaction.

In order for children to obtain maximum benefit from a mixed-age grouping, there should be ample opportunity for project work where children with different skill levels can work together. However, Katz et al. (1990) note the importance of also providing systematic instruction for individual children who may need to learn specific skills.

◆ ◆ ◆ ◆ The Interaction Between Family and Program

In both the United States and Canada, families whose children are enrolled in programs with different levels of quality have been found to differ in terms of:

◆ level of family stress, for example, parents work non-standard hours or the family is headed by a lone parent (Goelman & Pence, 1987; Howes & Olenick, 1986; Howes & Stewart, 1987; Kontos, 1991; White et al., 1992); and

◆ socioeconomic background, that is, the family's degree of advantage as measured by a combination of social factors and income (Goelman & Pence, 1987; Holloway & Reichhart-Erikson, 1988; Schliecker et al., 1991; Vandell et al., 1988; White, 1989; White et al., 1992).

The above studies indicate that children from less stressed families with higher socioeconomic status are more likely to be enrolled in high quality early childhood programs than are their peers from stressed and/or low socioeconomic status homes. Hypotheses put forward to explain these findings include the ability to pay for high quality care, the extent to which parents know what indicates quality in an early childhood program, and the possibility that parents under stress have less psychological energy available to compare different programs.

The above research findings raise three important issues:

◆ the extent to which the impact of the family and the early childhood program environment is additive;

◆ the impact of being from a family with a low socioeconomic status and also being enrolled in a poor quality early childhood program; and

◆ the possibility that a good quality early childhood program may compensate for some of the negative impact of low socioeconomic status or family stress.

The issue of the possible interaction between family setting and early childhood program has only recently begun to be explored by researchers. However, there are a few studies that provide some provocative information.

The possible additive factor

Three studies suggest that the impact of the home and the early childhood program may be additive. A Canadian study conducted in home-based child care found that the child's score on a standard test of language development was predicted by a combination of the language stimulation and the availability of toys and reading materials in *both* the child's home and the child care setting (Goelman & Pence, 1991). In the United States, Clarke-Stewart (1984) demonstrated that adding up the number of different kinds of toys in *both* the home and child care settings, or using *both* home and child care measures of the number of different kinds of toys, was more predictive of children's development than using either measures from the child's home or from the child care setting alone. Also in the United States, Howes & Olenick (1986) found that both the level of family stress and the quality of the early childhood program contributed to the prediction of the child's ability to keep focused on the task at hand and his or her ability to self-regulate. In this study, the impact of each of the two variables was controlled through a statistical procedure.

Poor quality programs and children from low socioeconomic backgrounds

As already discussed, the research on early childhood programs clearly links quality with child well-being and development. There is also a body of research that has demonstrated that children from low socioeconomic backgrounds have less developed language and cognitive skills than their peers from more advantaged families. This raises the question of the impact of being both enrolled in a poor quality program and being from a low socioeconomic status family. Schliecker et al. (1991), in a study conducted in Canada, compared same-age children from low socioeconomic status homes who were enrolled in child care centers with different total scores on the *Early Childhood Environment Rating Scale* (Harms & Clifford, 1980). They found that the children enrolled in poor quality child care had statistically significant lower scores on a standard test of language skills than did the children enrolled in high quality programs. This is only one study, but it suggests that children at risk of poorer development, because of their family background, may be at double jeopardy when enrolled in a poor quality early childhood program.

The possibility of compensation

A body of research has demonstrated the positive impact of special preschool compensatory programs for children at environmental risk (for example, Berrueta-Clement et al., 1984; Lazar & Darlington, 1982; Schweinhart et al., 1986). Few studies have looked at the possibility that an ordinary good quality program might compensate for some of the negative impact of low socioeconomic status or family stress. Howes et al. (1988), in the United States, found that security of attachment to both the mother and the child care provider was important in predicting the child's level of social competence. Those children with secure attachments to the care provider, but an insecure attachment to their mother, were less socially competent than children with secure attachments to both adults, but were more socially competent than children with an insecure attachment to both mother and caregiver. In Bermuda, McCartney et al. (1985) compared children from low income families, where the parents also had a low educational level, who were attending a high quality center with all the children of the same age attending eight other programs of varying quality. They found that the children in the high quality program obtained the highest scores on standard measures of language development and cognitive skills, as well as on measures of social competence. This is noteworthy since many of the children in the other programs came from homes with a higher socioeconomic status. While this is a study conducted outside North America, it is of interest since all nine programs were ordinary community settings with comparable levels of resources. These two studies suggest that positive experiences and attachments in an early childhood program may compensate for less positive experiences or relationships in the home.

❖ ❖ ❖ ❖ Implications for Practice

The possible additive impact of the child's home and the early childhood setting, and the body of research indicating that children from low socioeconomic status homes are more likely to be enrolled in poor quality child care, indicate the importance of assuring access to high quality early childhood programs for all children. This requires regulatory standards that go beyond simply trying to ensure that the child is safe and mechanisms to ensure that quality programs are financially accessible to low-income parents. White et al. (1992), in Canada, obtained information from 116 parents regarding which 5 out of 18 factors had most influenced their choice when selecting their child's current setting. They found that low socioeconomic status parents, whose children were also found to be most often in poor quality settings, were different from parents with higher socioeconomic status in only 2 of the 18 factors. These were cost and the availability of hours outside normal business hours, a factor that may have reflected the greater likelihood that these parents worked shifts. Parents with both low and higher socioeconomic status rated experienced, qualified staff, good supervision, a safe and clean environment, provision of nutritious food, caregivers who were warm and friendly with the children, and the availability of plenty of program materials among the most important reasons for their selection.

Glossary

A

Accreditation

A process by which a representative body, recognized by both the service community and the community in general, establishes standards for services. These standards are above the minimum regulatory requirements of government. Programs apply on a voluntary basis for evaluation against the standards and, if found to meet or surpass them, the program is granted a certificate that recognizes this fact.

Aimless wandering

The child is wandering around the setting in an unfocused fashion in contrast to being engaged in a focused, meaningful activity. This is considered to be undesirable behavior because it removes the child from opportunities to learn through interaction with other people or the environment.

Anti-bias programming (curriculum)

An approach that deliberately and actively rejects prejudice or bias in regard to gender, race, cultural background, socioeconomic status, religion, physical or mental ability, or sexual orientation. It encourages and assists children to explore the differences and similarities among individuals and groups, to develop a confident self-identity, and to challenge behaviors that are biased or discriminatory.

Auspices

The term "auspices" refers to who or what operates a program, for example, a voluntary board of directors.

Autism

A disability believed to be present at birth that is characterized by poor social skills, limited communication skills, a markedly restricted repertoire of activities, and the frequent repetition of specific activities.

B

Bias

An attitude or pre-judgment about specific groups of people, practices, or things, usually in favor of those that are familiar to the person and opposed to those that are unfamiliar.

C

Cerebral palsy

A disorder of the central nervous system resulting from brain damage before or during birth. It is characterized by defective motor ability that may also interfere with speech production.

Concurrent attendance

Enrollment in two programs at the same time, for example, in a kindergarten program in the morning and in a child care center in the afternoon.

Concurrent impact

The impact of the early childhood setting while the child is still in the program. This is in contrast to the long-term impact.

Concurrent research

Research that examines the impact of a program while the child is still enrolled in it.

Contextual factors

Those factors outside the individual program itself that have a direct effect on how it functions. These include factors such as the level of available funding and the regulations of the jurisdiction in which the program operates.

Control group

A group of people to whom subjects in an experiment are compared. The control group and the experimental subject group are matched on significant variables, such as age and socioeconomic status. The experimental group then receives a program or treatment that the control group does not. The two groups are compared to determine if the program or treatment had an impact on the experimental subjects.

Credentialing

A method to enable experienced child care staff, who have little or no formal education related to the provision of child care, to demonstrate that they have equivalent skills to those of a person with a diploma and/or certificate in early childhood education.

Culture

The total way of life of a group of people, including: their economic, family, religious, health, and educational systems; their form of government; and their way of viewing the world.

Custodial

A program that only addresses the health and safety of the children but is not designed to promote or encourage the development of skills.

D

Density

The number of square feet per child. High density refers to a relatively large number of children for the space available.

Detachment

An observed lack of involvement with the child by the adult who is supposed to be looking after the child, for example, an adult who passively watches a child but is not actively engaged with the child.

Developmental disability

A disability that manifests itself before age 18 months and limits the child's intellectual development. It may be accompanied by physical and/or sensory disabilities.

Developmentally appropriate practice

An approach to working with children that requires the adult to pay attention to what is appropriate to expect from, and do with, a child of a certain age, and what is appropriate for a specific child based on knowledge of that child's abilities, needs, background, and interests.

Disability

Impaired functioning as the result of an intellectual, sensory, or physical disorder.

Discrete perspective

An approach that focuses on only one aspect of a program. For example, a researcher studies the impact of adult responsiveness on children's language development.

Discrimination

Action taken or denied in regard to an individual or group on the basis of characteristics that are irrelevant to the issue or based on prejudice, for example, being denied a job because of skin color.

Diversity

A wide range. For example, a wide range of people of various appearances, abilities, ethnicity, culture, language, and religion.

Diversity education

An approach that includes multicultural education, anti-bias education, and anti-racist education.

Down Syndrome

A disability of genetic origin that limits the child's intellectual development.

E

Environmental risk

A situation where the child's normal development is put at risk due to factors such as: severe poverty, neglect, family violence, parental illness, or other parental stress.

G

Global perspective

An approach that looks at all, or a number of aspects of a situation, rather than focusing on a specific aspect. For example, when researchers look at the overall quality of a program, rather than focusing on individual characteristics, such as the number of children per adult, they are taking a global perspective.

Global rating

An evaluation based on a global perspective.

H

Harshness

Harsh behavior refers to being critical with the children, scolding or threatening them, or using punishment as a means of discipline.

Home-based child care

Child care by a non-relative provided in that person's own home.

I

Immune system

The presence of antibodies in the system that protect the person from disease. Infants have fewer antibodies than older children with the result that they are more vulnerable to bacterial and viral infections.

Incidence
The frequency with which something occurs.

Inclusion
The integration of a child with special needs into an ordinary program along with other children who do not have special needs.

L

Longitudinal study
Research that examines the effect of something on the same subject at several points in time. For example, a researcher might do a longitudinal study to investigate the effect of an early childhood program on children's language development and examine the same children's language skills when they were age four, age six, and age eight.

M

Mainstreaming
The integration of children who have disabilities into ordinary programs along with their non-disabled peers.

Maturation
Growth that results simply from the passage of time rather than as the result of deliberate efforts. For example, children move from the stage of babbling to beginning to use clearly articulated words purely on the basis of maturation.

Mean
A statistical term that refers to the average score on a variable. It is calculated by taking the sum of all the scores on the variable and dividing it by the total number of subjects.

Mixed-age group
A group that includes people more than one year of age apart. For example, a group of toddlers and preschoolers.

Model, modeling
When deliberate, modeling refers to the use of another person to show, by example, how something is done. Modeling also occurs spontaneously when a child observes a more competent peer and then mimics what the peer does.

Multicultural education
Programming specifically designed to support diversity of race, culture, language, and religion as a natural and positive human experience.

N

Native
A general term for a person who is a descendant of one of the original inhabitants of North America. Other general terms are: Aboriginal person, First Nations person, Inuit, and Native American.

P

Peer
A child of the same or similar age to the child in question.

Positive adult interaction
Adult behavior with and towards children that is characterized by active interest in the children and high levels of encouragement and involvement.

Predict
Predict refers to the situation where knowledge of one variable enables an accurate estimate of what will occur with another variable. For example, several studies have found a statistically significant relationship (that is, one that could not happen by chance) between level and type of staff training and the level of the children's language skills in the program studied. Thus, in the situations where the studies occurred, knowledge of the adult's level and type of training enabled prediction of the level of the language development in the children they are working with.

Preoperational stage (Piagetian theory)
A period of cognitive development during which the child is limited to concrete understanding of the environment obtained through direct involvement and manipulation.

Pre-prejudice
Discomfort with people who are different from you, especially if the difference is in regard to race, ethnicity, or culture.

Prejudice

An opinion about an individual or a group that is based on assumptions rather than actual knowledge. Usually prejudice is a negative attitude.

Preschooler

The period between being a toddler and entering grade one, usually at age six. The definition of the toddler period is somewhat variable in the research literature. However, the preschool period can be thought to begin between age 18 months and two years.

R

Ratio

The number of children for whom an adult is responsible. For example, a staff-to-child ratio of 1:8 means one adult is responsible for eight children.

Regulatory status

Refers to whether or not a program has met specific government standards and been given a license or permit to operate.

Reinforcement

The rewarding of desired behavior.

Responsiveness

Adult behavior that is characterized by reacting appropriately and promptly to the child's verbal or non-verbal signals for attention. It includes having expectations that are appropriate for the child's age, providing activities that are age-appropriate, and being sensitive to the child's current mood.

Restrictiveness

Adult behavior that controls and limits the child's activities to an inappropriate degree.

S

Sample representiveness

The extent to which the sample studied is an accurate reflection of the total population. For example, a sample of 20-year-old college students must include both men and women in order to be representative of 20-year-old college students in general.

Secure attachment

The type of relationship between child and adult in which the child feels able to rely on the emotional and physical availability of the adult to provide assistance if required.

Self-concept

A person's definition of self. For example, as being competent or as being clumsy and incompetent.

Significant, or statistically significant

A statistical term that identifies the extent to which the relationship between two items, for example, between adult responsiveness and child social skills, is likely to have occurred by chance. If a relationship is significant at the .05 level, the lowest level accepted as being significant, it means that the probability of the relationship having occurred by chance is 5 in 100. Within the scientific community, the .05 level is considered to indicate that one item, for example, child social skills, is the result of another, for example, adult responsiveness.

Socialization agent

A person who teaches a less experienced person what behaviors, forms of address, and so on are expected in a particular social environment.

Socioeconomic status

The individual's or family's degree of advantage as measured by a combination of social factors, such as level of education and income.

Special needs

A child is considered to have special needs when the child requires help and information beyond what is normally required by a child of the same age in order to assure the best developmental outcome.

Sponsorship

In some jurisdictions, home-based child care providers operate under the sponsorship of an agency or municipal government. The sponsor is licensed by the state, province, or territory and is expected to provide the caregiver with regular in-home visits, training, and other forms of support.

Staff consistency

The extent to which staff members remain employed at the same program or continue to look after the same group of children.

Staff-to-child ratio
The number of children for whom a single adult is responsible. A staff-to-child ratio of 1:8 means than one adult is responsible for eight children.

Staff turnover rate
The frequency with which staff leave a program. It is usually expressed as a percentage and measured on the basis of the number of people who leave in a 12-month period.

Statistically significant relationship
See above notation for significant.

Stereotype
An image of an individual or group based on certain characteristics, real or imagined, and applied equally to all members of the group without regard to actual characteristics or individual differences. For example, the stereotype that all Italians love opera and are good singers.

Structural features
Those features of an early childhood program that are observable and can be easily regulated, for example, staff-to-child ratio, class size, and staff training level.

T

Transdisciplinary approach or team
The involvement of two or more people from different disciplines to assess, and/or develop an intervention plan for, and/or implement an intervention plan with, a child who has special needs. For example, a transdisciplinary team might include a child care center worker, a physiotherapist, and a psychologist.

Transfer (as in transfer of skills)
The ability to use a learned skill in a setting other than the setting in which the skill was learned.

V

Variance
A statistical term that refers to the extent to which members of a group differ from each other.

Verbal exchange
A two-way verbal communication, as in a conversation, in contrast to the one-way situation when an adult instructs a child to do something.

Visible minority
In general usage, this term refers to a person who is of Native, African, East Indian, or Asian origin.

Z

Zone of proximal growth
The hypothesized area of cognitive competence within which the child cannot solve problems alone but can in cooperation with a person of greater cognitive competence.

References

Ainslie, R.C., & Anderson, C. (1984). Daycare children's relationships to their mothers and caregivers: An inquiry into the conditions of the development of attachment. In R.C. Ainslie (Ed.), *The child and the day care setting: Qualitative variations and development*. New York: Praeger, 98-132.

Allhusen, V.D., & Cochran, M.M. (1991). Infant attachment behaviours with their day care providers. Paper presented at the biennial meeting of the Society for Research in Child Development. ED 338 406.

American Academy of Pediatrics. (1992). *National health and safety performance standards for out of home child care programs*. Elkgrove Village, Illinois: Author.

Anderson, C.W., Nagle, R.J., Roberts, W.A., & Smith, J.W. (1981). Attachment to substitute caregivers as a function of center quality and caregiver involvement. *Child Development*, 52, 53-61.

Andersson, B-E. (1989). Effects of public day care: A longitudinal study. *Child Development*, 60, 857-866.

Andersson, B-E. (1992). Effects of day care on cognitive and socioemotional development of thirteen-year-old Swedish children. *Child Development*, 63, 20-26.

Arnett, J. (1989). Caregivers in day care centers: Does training matter? *Developmental Psychology*, 10, 541-552.

Association for Early Childhood Education, Ontario. (1986). *A regional analysis of Canada's national child care subsidy system: Salaries and work experience in the Municipality of Hamilton-Wentworth*. Hamilton, Ontario: Author.

Atten, D.W., & Milner, J.S. (1987). Child abuse potential and work satisfaction in day care employees. *Child Abuse & Neglect*, 11, 117-123.

Belsky, J., & Steinberg, C.D. (1978). The effects of day care: A critical review. *Child Development*, 49, 929-949.

Berk, L. (1985). Relationship of caregiver education to child-oriented attitudes, job satisfaction, and behaviors towards children. *Child Care Quarterly*, 14(2), 103-129.

Berrueta-Clement, J.R., Schweinhart, L.J., Barnett, W.S., Epstein, A.S., & Weikart, D.P. (1984). *Changed lives: The effects of the Perry Preschool Program on youths through age 19*. Ypsilanti, Michigan: High Scope Press.

Betsalel-Presser, R., Joncas, M., Jacques, M., Phaneuf, J., Rivest, E., & Brunet, C. (1991). *Is communication among kindergarten teachers and school care educators an issue?* Paper presented at the Annual Conference of the Canadian Society for the Study of Education. Kingston, Ontario.

Biemiller, A., Avis, C., & Lindsay, A. (1976). *Competence supporting aspects of day care environments*. Paper presented at the Canadian Psychological Convention. Toronto, Ontario.

Black, R.E., Dykes, A.C., Anderson, K.E., Wells, J.G., Sinclair, S.P., Gary, G.W., Hatch, M.H., & Gangarosa, E.J. (1981). Handwashing to prevent diarrhea in day care centers. *American Journal of Epidemiology*, 113(4), 445-451.

Bowlby, J. (1969/1982). *Attachment and loss* (2nd edition). New York: Basic Books.

Bredekamp, S. (1987). *Developmentally appropriate practice in early childhood programs serving children from birth through age 8*. Washington, D.C.: National Association for the Education of Young Children.

Bredekamp, S. (1991). Redeveloping early childhood education: A response to Kessler. *Early Childhood Research Quarterly*, 6(2), 199-209.

Bredekamp, S. (1993). Myths about developmentally appropriate practice: A response to Fowell and Lawton. *Early Childhood Research Quarterly*, 8(1), 117-119.

Bredekamp, S. (undated). *Regulating child care quality: Evidence from NAEYC's accreditation system*. Washington, D.C: National Association for the Education of Young Children.

Bredekamp, S., & Rosegrant, T. (1992). Reaching potentials: Introduction. In S. Bredekamp & T. Rosegrant (Eds.), *Reaching potentials: Appropriate curriculum and assessment for young children*. Washington, D.C: National Association for the Education of Young Children, 2-8.

Broberg, A., & Hwang, C-P. (1991). Day care for young children in Sweden. In E.C. Melhuish & P. Moss (Eds.), *Day care for young children: International perspectives*. London, England: Tavistock/Routledge, 75-101.

Broberg, A., Lamb, M.E., Hwang, C-P., & Bookstein, F.L. (1989a). Factors related to verbal abilities in Swedish preschoolers. In A. Broberg (Ed.), *Child care and early development*. Goteborg, Sweden: Department of Psychology, University of Goteborg, Part III.

Broberg, A., Lamb, M.E., Hwang, C-P., & Ketterlinus, R.D. (1989b). Child care effects on socioemotional and intellectual competence in Swedish preschoolers. In A. Broberg (Ed.), *Child care and early development*. Goteborg, Sweden: Psychology Department, University of Goteborg, Part IV.

Bryant, D.M., Clifford, R.M., & Peisner, E.S. (1991). Best practices for beginners: Developmental appropriateness in kindergarten. *American Educational Research Journal*, 28(4), 783-803.

Burchinal, M., Lee, M., & Ramey, C. (1989). Type of day care and preschool intellectual development in disadvantaged children. *Child Development*, 60, 128-137.

Burts, D.C., Hart, C.H., Charlesworth, R., Fleege, P.O., Mosley, J., & Thomasson, R.H. (1992). Observed activities and stress behaviors of children in developmentally appropriate and inappropriate kindergarten classrooms. *Early Childhood Research Quarterly*, 7(2), 297-318.

California State Department of Education. (1988). *Program quality review instruments* (infant, preschool, school-age). Sacramento, California: Child Development Division.

Canadian Child Care Federation/Canadian Child Care Advocacy Association. (1992). *Caring for a living*. Ottawa, Ontario: Canadian Child Care Federation.

Canadian Child Day Care Federation. (1993). *National Statement on Quality Child Care*. Ottawa, Ontario: Author.

Canadian Paediatric Society. (1992). *Well-beings: A guide to promote the physical health, safety and emotional well-being of children in child care centres and family day care homes*, Vol. 1 and 2. Ottawa, Ontario: Author.

Canning, P.M. (1986). The Nairn daycare project. *Canadian Journal of Education*, 11(1), 1-8.

Canning, P.M., & Lyon, M.E. (1990). Young children with special needs. In I.M. Doxey (Ed.), *Child care and education: Canadian dimensions*. Scarborough, Ontario: Nelson Canada, 254-268.

Carew, J. (1979). *Observation study of caregiver and children in day care homes.* Paper presented at the Society for Research in Child Development meeting. San Francisco, California.

Carew, J. (1980). Experience and the development of intelligence in young children at home and in day care. *Monographs of the Society for Research in Child Development,* 45 (6-7, Serial No. 187).

Chud, G., & Fahlman, R. (1985). *Early childhood education for a multicultural society.* Vancouver, B.C.: Pacific Education Press.

Clarke-Stewart, K.A. (1987). Predicting child development from childcare forms and features: The Chicago Study. In D. Phillips (Ed.), *Quality in child care: What does the research tell us?* Washington, D.C: National Association for the Education of Young Children, 21-41.

Clarke-Stewart, K.A., & Gruber, C.P. (1984). Day care forms and features. In R. Ainslie (Ed.), *The child and the day care setting: Qualitative variations and development.* New York: Praeger, 35-62.

Cloutier, R. (1985). Pourquoi des parents à la garderie? *Petit à Petit,* 3(6), 22-24.

Coie, J.D., & Dodge, K.A. (1983). Continuities and changes in children's social status: A five-year longitudinal study. *Merrill-Palmer Quarterly,* 29, 261-282.

Coie, J.D., & Kupersmidt, J. (1983). A behavioral analysis of emerging social status in boys' groups. *Child Development,* 54, 1406-1416.

Cooke, T.P., & Ruskus, J.A., Appolloni, T., & Peck, C.A. (1981). Handicapped preschool children in the mainstream: Background, outcomes, and clinical suggestions. *Topics in Early Childhood Special Education,* 1(1), 73-83.

Cooper, L. (1994). Winnipeg, Manitoba: Child Day Care Branch, Department of Family Services, personal communication.

Cowen, E.L., Pederson, A., Babigan, H., Izzo, L.D., & Trost, M.A. (1973). Long-term follow-up of early detected vulnerable children. *Journal of Consulting and Clinical Psychology,* 41, 438-446.

Cummings, E.M. (1980). Caregiver stability and day care. *Developmental Psychology,* 16(1), 31-37.

Cummins, J. (1986). Empowering minority students: A framework for intervention. *Harvard Educational Review,* 56, 18-26.

DeGagné, C., & Gagné, M-P. (1988). *Garderies à but lucratif et garderies sans but lucratif subventionnées vers une évaluation de la qualité.* Montréal, Québec: Government of Québec, l'Office des services en garde à l'enfance.

Derman-Sparks, L., & the A.B.C. Task Force. (1989). *Anti-bias curriculum: Tools for empowering young children.* Washington, DC: National Association for the Education of Young Children.

Derman-Sparks, L., Higa, C.T., & Sparks, B. (1990). Children, race, and racism: How race awareness develops. In K.M. Kilbride (Ed.), *Multicultural early childhood education training program.* Trainer's manual. Handout No. 5.2. Toronto, Ontario: Ryerson Polytechnic University.

Division for Early Childhood of the Council for Exceptional Children. (1993). *DEC recommended practices: Indicators of quality in programs for infants and young children with special needs and their families.* Reston, Va: Author.

Dodge, K. (1983). Behavioral antecedents of peer social status. *Child Development*, 54, 1386-1399.

Doherty, G. (1991). *Factors related to quality in child care: A review of the literature.* Toronto, Ontario: Ministry of Community and Social Services.

Doherty, G. (1994). *Rural child care in Ontario.* Toronto: The Childcare Resource and Research Unit, Centre for Urban and Community Studies, University of Toronto.

Doyle, A.B., Connolly, J.A., & Rivest, L. (1980). The effect of playmate familiarity on the social interactions of young children. *Child Development*, 51, 217-223.

Dunn, L.M. (1979). *The Peabody Picture Vocabulary Test.* Circle Pines, Minnesota: American Guidance Service.

Elkind, D. (1987). Early childhood education on its own terms. In S. Kagan & E. Zigler (Eds.), *Early schooling: The national debate.* New Haven, Conn: Yale University Press, 98-115.

Endsley, R. C., & Minish, P.A. (1991). Parent-staff communication in day care centers during morning and afternoon transitions. *Early Childhood Research Quarterly*, 6(2), 119-135.

Erikson, E.H. (1963). *Childhood and society*, 2nd edition. New York: Norton.

Fewell, R.R., & Oelwein, P.L. (1990). The relationship between time in integrated environments and developmental gains in young children with special needs. *Topics in Early Childhood Special Education*, 10(2), 104-116.

Field, T. (1980). Preschool play: effects of teacher-child ratio and organization of classroom space. *Child Study Journal*, 10(3), 191-205.

Fiene, R., & Melnick, S.A. (1990). *Licensure and program quality in early childhood and childcare programs.* Paper presented at the American Educational Research Association annual convention. Boston, Mass.

File, N., & Kontos, S. (1992). Indirect service delivery through consultation: Review and implications for early intervention. *Journal of Early Intervention*, 16(2), 221-233.

Fischer, J.L., & Eheart, B.K. (1991). Family day care: A theoretical basis for improving quality. *Early Childhood Research Quarterly*, 6(4), 549-563.

Fosburg, S. (1981). *Family day care in the United States. Final Report of the National Day Care Home Study,* Volume I. Cambridge, Mass: Abt Associates.

Frankel, E.B. (1988). Resource teacher: A segregated or integrated experience? *Resources in Early Childhood Education*, 3, 3-5.

Frankel, E.B. (1994). *Resource teachers in integrated children's centres: Implications for staff development.* Unpublished document. Toronto, Ontario: Ryerson Polytechnic University.

Frankel, E.B., & McKay, D. (1990). *An interactive model of integration in community-based child care centres.* Presented at the 68th Annual Conference of the Council for Exceptional Children. Toronto, Ontario. ED 334 774.

Friesen, B.K. (1992). *A sociological examination of the effects of auspice on day care quality.* Ph.D. dissertation. Calgary, Alberta: Department of Sociology, University of Calgary.

Gagné, M-P. (1989). *Participation des parents aux services de garde.* Montréal, Québec: Government of Québec, l'Office des services de garde à l'enfance.

Galinsky, E. (1988). Parents and teacher-caregivers: Sources of tension, sources of support. *Young Children,* 43(3), 4-12.

Galinsky, E., Howes, C., Kontos, S., & Shinn, M. (1994). *The study of children in family child care and relative care.* New York: Families and Work Institute.

Gehlbach, S.H., MacCormack, J.N., Drake, B.M., & Thompson, W.V. (1973). Spread of disease by fecal-oral route in day nurseries. *Health Service Reports,* 88, 320-322.

Goelman, H., & Pence, A.R. (1987). Effects of child care, family, and individual characteristics on children's language development: The Victoria day care research project. In D. Phillips (Ed.), *Quality in child care: What does the research tell us?* Washington, D.C.: National Association for the Education of Young Children, 89-104.

Goelman, H., & Pence, A.R. (1988). Children in three types of child care experiences: Quality of care and developmental outcomes. *Early Childhood Development and Care,* 33, 67-76.

Goelman, H., & Pence, A.R. (1991). Talking to children: The effects of the home and the family day care environment. *Proceedings from the Child Care Policy and Research Symposium.* Kingston, Ontario. Toronto: Childcare Resource and Research Unit, University of Toronto. Occasional Paper No. 2, 63-88.

Golden, M., Rosenbluth, L., Grossi, M., Policare, H., Freeman, H., & Brownlees, E. (1979). *The New York City Infant Day Care Study.* New York: Medical and Health Research Association of New York City, Inc.

Goldman, J. (1981). Social participation of preschool children in same- versus mixed-aged groups. *Child Development,* 52, 644-650.

Goldstein, H., Wickstrom, S., Hoyson, M., Jamieson, B., & Odom, S. (1988). Effects of sociodramatic script training on social and communicative interaction. *Education and the Treatment of Children,* 11(2), 97-117.

Goodman, N., & Andrews, J. (1981). Cognitive development of children in family and group day care. *American Journal of Orthopsychiatry,* 51(2), 271-284.

Goossens, F.A., & van IJzendoorn, M.H. (1990). Quality of infants' attachments to professional caregivers: Relation to infant-parent attachment and day care characteristics. *Child Development,* 61, 832-837.

Guralnick, M.J. (1982). Programmatic factors affecting child-child social interactions in mainstreamed preschool programs. In P.S. Strain (Ed.), *Social development in exceptional children.* Rockville, MD: Aspen, 71-92.

Guralnick, M.J., and Groom, J. (1988). Peer interaction in mainstreamed and specialized classrooms. *Exceptional Children,* 54, 415-425.

Haddock, M.D., & McQueen, W.M. (1983). Assessing employee potential for abuse. *Journal of Clinical Psychology,* 39(6), 1021-1029.

Halder, S.C., Erben, J.J., Francis, D.P., Webster, H.M., & Maynard, J.E. (1982). Risk factors for hepatitis A in day care centers. *The Journal of Infectious Diseases,* 145(2), 255-261.

Halder, S.C., & McFarland, L. (1986). Hepatitis in day care centers: Epidemiology and prevention. *Review of Infectious Diseases,* 8, 548-557.

Hanline, M.F. (1985). Integrating disabled children. *Young Children,* 40(2), 45-58.

Hanson, M.J. (1990). Honoring the cultural diversity of families when gathering data. *Topics in Early Childhood Special Education,* 10(2), 112-131.

Hanson, M.J., & Widerstrom, A.H. (1993). Consultation and collaboration: Essentials for integration efforts for young children. In C.A. Peck, S.L. Odom, & D.D. Bricker (Eds.), *Integrating young children with disabilities into community programs*. Baltimore, MA: Paul Brookes Publishing Co., 149-168.

Harms, T., & Clifford, R.M. (1980). *Early Childhood Environment Rating Scale*. New York: Teachers College Press, Columbia University.

Harms, T., & Clifford, R.M. (1986). *Infant/toddler Environment Rating Scale*. Unpublished document. Chapel Hill, North Carolina: University of North Carolina.

Harms, T., & Clifford, R.M. (1989). *Family Day Care Rating Scale*. New York: Teachers College Press, Columbia University.

Harms, T., Clifford, R.M., & Padan-Belkin, E. (1983). *The Day Care Home Environment Rating Scale*. Chapel Hill, North Carolina: University of North Carolina.

Harms, T., Cryer, D., & Clifford, R.M. (1990). *Infant/toddler Environment Rating Scale*. New York: Teachers College Press, Columbia University.

Hartman, H., & Pearce, D. (1989). *High skill and low pay: The economics of child care work*. New York: Child Care Action Campaign.

Haskins, R. (1985). Public aggression among children with varying day care experience. *Child Development*, 56, 689-703.

Hatch, J.A., & Freeman, E.G. (1988). Kindergarten philosophies and practices: Perspectives of teachers, principals, and supervisors. *Early Childhood Research Quarterly*, 3, 151-166.

Hayes, C.D., Palmer, J.L., & Zaslow, M.J. (1990). *Who cares for America's children: Child care policy for the 1990s*. Washington, D.C.: National Research Council, Panel on Child Care Policy, National Academy Press.

Health and Welfare Canada. (1994). *Status of day care in Canada 1992*. Ottawa: National Child Care Information Centre, Child Care Programs Division.

Henrickson, J.M., Strain, P.S., Tremblay, A., & Shores, R.E. (1981). Relationship between toy and material use and the occurrence of social interaction behaviors in normally developing preschool children. *Psychology in the Schools*, 18(4), 500-504.

Hilgendorf, L. (1984). Transmitting tribal traditions. *Children Today*, 14 (Sept./Oct.), 30-32.

Hofferth, S., Brayfield, A., Deich, S., & Holcomb, P. (1991). *National child care survey, 1990*. Washington, DC: The Urban Institute Press.

Hogan, E.L. (1991). *The importance of the mother-provider relationship in family child care homes*. Paper presented at the Midwest Regional Conference of the Association for the Education of Young Children. Des Moines. ED 340 470.

Holloway, S.D., & Reichhart-Erikson, M. (1988). The relationship of day care quality to children's free play behavior and social problem solving skills. *Early Childhood Research Quarterly*, 3, 39-53.

Howes, C. (1983). Caregiver behavior in center and in family day care. *Journal of Applied Developmental Psychology*, 4, 99-107.

Howes, C. (1986). *Quality indicators for infant-toddler care*. Paper presented at the annual meeting of the American Educational Research Foundation. San Francisco. ED 273 385.

Howes, C. (1987). Social competency with peers: Contributions from child care. *Early Childhood Research Quarterly*, 2(2), 155-167.

Howes, C. (1988). Relations between early child care and schooling. *Developmental Psychology*, 24(1), 53-57.

Howes, C. (1990). Can the age of entry into child care and the quality of child care predict adjustment in kindergarten? *Developmental Psychology*, 26(2), 1-12.

Howes, C., & Farver, S.A. (1987). Social pretend play in two-year olds: Effect of age of partner. *Early Childhood Research Quarterly*, 2, 305-314.

Howes, C., & Hamilton, C.E. (1992). Children's relationships with caregivers: Mothers and child care teachers. *Child Development*, 63, 859-866.

Howes, C., & Hamilton, C.E. (1993). The changing experience of child care: Changes in teachers and in teacher-child relationships. *Early Childhood Research Quarterly*, 8(1), 15-32.

Howes, C., & Olenick, M. (1986). Family and child care influences on toddler's compliance. *Child Development*, 57, 202-216.

Howes, C., Phillips, D.A., & Whitebook, M. (1992). Thresholds of quality: Implications for the social development of children in center-based care. *Child Development*, 63(4), 449-460.

Howes, C., Rodning, C., Galluzzo, D.C., & Myers, L. (1988). Attachment and child care: Relationships with mother and caregiver. *Early Childhood Research Quarterly*, 14(2), 140-151.

Howes, C., & Rubenstein, J. (1981). Toddler peer behavior in two types of day care. *Infant Behavior and Development*, 4, 387-393.

Howes, C., & Rubenstein, J. (1985). Determinants of toddlers' experiences in day care: Age of entry and quality of setting. *Child Care Quarterly*, 14(2), 140-151.

Howes, C., & Stewart, P. (1987). Child's play with adults, toys, and peers: An examination of family and child care influences. *Developmental Psychology*, 23(3), 423-430.

Irwin, S.H. (1993). *The SpeciaLink book: On the road to mainstream daycare*. Wreck Cove, Nova Scotia: Breton Books.

Jacobs, E., Selig, G., & White, D.R. (1992). Classroom behaviour in grade one: Does quality of preschool experience make a difference? *Canadian Journal of Research in Early Childhood Education*, 3(2), 89-100.

Jenkins, J.R., Odom, S.L., & Speltz, M.L. (1989). Effects of social integration on preschool children with handicaps. *Exceptional Children*, 55, 420-428.

Johnson, J.S., & Newport, E.L. (1989). Critical period effects in second language learning: The influence of maturational state on the acquisition of English as a second language. *Cognitive Psychology*, 21, 60-69.

Jones, S.N., & Meisels, S.J. (1987). Training family day care providers to work with special needs children. *Topics in Early Childhood Special Education*, 7(1), 1-12.

Jorde-Bloom, P. (1988). *A great place to work: Improving conditions for staff in young children's programs*. Washington, D.C: National Association for the Education of Young Children.

Jorde-Bloom, P. (1989). *The Illinois Director's Study*. Report submitted to the Illinois Department of Children and Family Services. Evanston, Illinois: National College of Education. ED 305 167.

Kagan, S.L., & Newton, J.W. (1989). For-profit and non-profit child care: similarities and differences. *Young Children*, November, 4-10.

Kamerman, S. (1989). Child care, women, work, and the family: An international overview of child care services and related policies. In J.S. Lande, S.Scarr, N. Gunzenhauser (Eds.), *Caring for children: Challenge for America*. Hillsdale, N.J: Erlbaum, 93-110.

Kaplan, M.G., & Conn, J.S. (1984). The effects of caregiver training on classroom setting and caregiver performance in eight community day care centers. *Child Study Journal*, 14(2), 79-93.

Katz, L. (1987). Early education: What should young children be doing? In S. Kagan & E. Zigler (Eds.), *Early schooling: The national debate*. New Haven, Conn: Yale University Press, 151-167.

Katz, L. (1992). *Mixed-age grouping in early childhood programs*. Urbana, Illinois: ERIC Clearing House on Elementary and Early Childhood Education. ED 351 148.

Katz, L. (1993). *Five perspectives on quality in early childhood programs*. Perspectives from ERIC/EECE. A monograph series, No. 1. Urbana, Illinois: ERIC Clearing House on Elementary and Early Childhood Education.

Katz, L., Evangelou, D., & Hartman, J.A. (1990). *The case for mixed-age grouping in early childhood*. Washington, D.C: National Association for the Education of Young Children. ED 326 302.

Kendall, F.E. (1983). *Diversity in the classroom: A multicultural approach to the education of young children*. New York: Teachers College Press.

Kilbride, K.M. (1990). *Multicultural early childhood education: A resource kit*. Toronto, Ontario: Ryerson Polytechnic University.

Klein, J.O. (1986). Infectious diseases and day care. In M.T. Osterholm, J.O. Klein, S.S. Aronson, & L.K. Pickering (Eds.), *Infectious diseases in child day care: Management and prevention*. Chicago, Illinois: University of Chicago Press, 9-13.

Kontos, S. (1988). Family day care as an integrated early intervention setting. *Topics in Early Childhood Special Education*, 8, 1-14.

Kontos, S. (1990). *Children, families, and child care: The search for connections*. Paper presented at the annual meeting of the American Educational Research Association.

Kontos, S. (1991). Child care quality, family background, and children's development. *Early Childhood Research Quarterly*, 6(2), 249-262.

Kontos, S., & Fiene, R. (1986). *Predictors of quality and children's development in day care*. Unpublished manuscript. Harrisburg, Pennsylvania: Pennsylvania State University.

Kontos, S., & Fiene, R. (1987). Child care quality: compliance with regulations and children's development: The Pennsylvania Study. In D. Phillips (Ed.), *Quality in child care: What does the research tell us*? Washington, D.C: National Association for the Education of Young Children, 57-79.

Kontos, S., & Stevens, A.J. (1985). High quality day care: Does your center measure up? *Young Children*, 40(2), 5-9.

Kontos, S., & Stremmel, A.J. (1988). Caregiver's perceptions of working conditions in a child care environment. *Early Childhood Research Quarterly*, 3, 77-90.

Lamb, M.E., Hwang, C-P., Broberg, A., & Bookstein, F.L. (1988). The effects of out-of-home care on the development of social competence in Sweden: A longitudinal study. *Early Childhood Research Quarterly*, 3, 379-402.

Lazar, I., & Darlington, R. (1982). *Lasting effects of early education: A report from the Consortium for Longitudinal Studies*. Monograph of the Society for Research in Child Development, No. 195.

Lee, G. (1989). *Letters to Marcia: A teacher's guide to anti-racist education.* Ontario: Cross Cultural Communication Centre.

Lemp, G.F., Woodward, W.E., Pickering, L.K., Sullivan, P.S., & Dupont, H.L. (1984). The relationship of staff to the incidence of diarrhea in day care centers. *American Journal of Epidemiology*, 120, 750-758.

Love, J.M. (1993). *Does children's behavior reflect day care classroom quality?* Paper presented at the biennial meeting of the Society for Research in Child Development. New Orleans. ED 356 085.

Love, J.M., Nanta, M.J., Coelen, C.G., Hewlett, K., & Ruopp, R.R. (1976). *National Home Start evaluation*. Cambridge, MA: Abt Associates.

Maslach, C., & Pines, A. (1977) The burn-out syndrome in the day care setting. *Child Care Quarterly*, 6(2), 100-113.

Mayfield, M. (1990). Parent involvement in early childhood programs. In I.M. Doxey (Ed.), *Child care and education: Canadian dimensions.* Scarborough, Ontario: Nelson Canada, 240-253.

McCartney, K. (1984). Effect of quality of day care environment on children's language development. *Developmental Psychology*, 20(2), 244-260.

McCartney, K., Scarr, S., Phillips, D.A., & Grajek, S. (1985). Day care as an intervention: Comparisons of varying quality programs. *Journal of Applied Developmental Psychology*, 6, 247-260.

McCartney, K., Scarr, S., Phillips, D., Grajek, S., & Schwartz, J.C. (1982). Environmental differences among day care centers and their effects on children's development. In E.F. Zigler & G. W. Gordon (Eds.), *Day care scientific and social policy issues.* Boston, Mass: Auburn, 126-151.

McClellan, D. (1991). *Children's social behavior as related to participation in mixed-age or same-age groups.* Ph.D. dissertation. Urbana, Champagne: University of Illinois.

McClellan, D. (1993). *Research on mixed-age grouping: Implications for education.* Paper presented at the Third European Conference on the Quality of Early Childhood Education. Thesolonika, Greece.

McLean, M. (1990). Providing early intervention services in integrated environments: Challenges and opportunities for the future. *Topics in Early Childhood Special Education*, 10(2), 62-77.

McLean, M., & Odom, S.L. (1993). Practices for young children with and without disabilities: A comparison of DEC and NAEYC identified practices. *Topics in Early Childhood Special Education*, 13(3), 274-292.

Melhuish, E.C., Mooney, A., Martin, S., & Lloyd, E. (1990a). Type of childcare at 18 months — I. Differences in interactional experience. *Journal of Child Psychology & Psychiatry*, 31(6), 849-859.

Melhuish, E.C., Mooney, A., Martin, S., & Lloyd, E., (1990b). Type of childcare at 18 months — II . Relations with cognitive and language development. *Journal of Child Psychology & Psychiatry*, 31(6), 861-870.

Mock, K. (1982). Early education in a multicultural society. *Multiculturalism*, 5(4), 3-6.

Mock, K. (1989). *Parents' needs for and perceptions of early childhood education in Ontario*. Unpublished document. Toronto, Ontario: Ontario Ministry of Community and Social Services, Child Care Branch.

Moore, B.F., Snow, C.W., & Poteat, G.M. (1988). Effects of variant types of child care experience on the adaptive behavior of kindergarten children. *American Journal of Orthopsychiatry*, 58(2), 297-303.

Moore, G.T. (1986). Effects of the spatial definition of behavior settings on children's behavior: A quasi-experimental field study. *Journal of Environmental Psychology*, 6, 205-231.

Moore, G.T. (1987). The physical environment and cognitive development in child care centers. In C.S. Weinstein & T.G. David (Eds.), *Spaces for children: The built environment and child development*. New York: Plenum Press, 41-72.

Morgan, G. (1979). Regulation: One approach to quality child care. *Young Children*, 34(6), 22-27.

Morgan, G. (1980). Can quality family day care be achieved through regulation? In S. Kilmer (Ed.), *Advances in early education and day care*, Vol. I. Grenwich, Conn: JAI Press, 77-102.

Moyer, J., Egerston, H., & Isenberg, J. (1987). The child-centred kindergarten. *Childhood Education*, 64, 235-242.

Mueller, E., & Vandell, D.L. (1979). Infant-infant interaction: A review. In J.D. Osofsky (Ed.), *Handbook of infant development*. New York: Wiley-Interscience, 591-622.

National Academy of Early Childhood Programs. (1984). *Criteria for high quality early childhood programs with interpretations*. Washington, DC: National Association for the Education of Young Children.

National Association for the Education of Young Children. (1983). Four components of high quality early childhood programs: Staff-child interaction, child-child interaction, curriculum, and evaluation. *Young Children*, 38(6), 46-52.

Nelson, M.J. (1989). *Does training make a difference?* ED 309 873.

Newport, E.L. (1988). Constraints on learning and their role in language acquisition. *Language Sciences*, 10, 147-172.

Notari, A., & Cole, K. (1993). Language intervention: Research and implication for service delivery. In C.A. Peck, S.L. Odom, & D.D. Bricker (Eds.), *Integrating young children into community programs*. Baltimore, MA: Paul Brookes Publishing Co., 17-38.

Odom, S.L., & Brown, W.H. (1993). Social interaction skills interventions for young children with disabilities in integrated settings. In C.A. Peck, S.L. Odom, & D.D. Bricker (Eds.), *Integrating young children with disabilities into community programs*. Baltimore, MA: Paul Brookes Publishing Co., 39-64.

Odom, S.L., & McEvoy, M.A. (1988). Integration of young children with handicaps and normally developing children. In S.L. Odom & M.B. Karnes (Eds.), *Early intervention for infants and children with handicaps: An empirical base*. Baltimore: Paul H. Brooks Publishing, 241-267.

Ooms, T., & Herendeen, L. (1989). *Quality in child care: What is it and how should it be encouraged?* Family Impact Seminar, Washington, D.C. ED 345 851.

Palmerus, K. (1991). The impact of ratio of children/caregiver on social interaction and activity pattern in a day care center. *Early Child Development and Care,* 71, 97-103.

Parker, J.C., & Asher, S.R. (1987). Peer relations and later social adjustment: Are low accepted children at risk? *Psychology Bulletin,* 102, 357-389.

Pence, A.R., & Goelman, H. (undated). *Can you see the difference? Regulation, training, and quality of care in family day care.* Unpublished document. Victoria, B.C: University of Victoria.

Pence, A.R., & Goelman, H. (1987). Silent partners: Parents of children in three types of day care. *Early Childhood Research Quarterly,* 2(2), 103-118.

Pence, A.R., & Goelman, H. (1991). The relationship of regulation, training and motivation to quality of care in family day care. *Child and Youth Care Forum,* 20(2), 83-101.

Pepper, S., & Stuart, B. (1992). Quality of family day care in licensed and unlicensed homes. *Canadian Journal of Research in Early Childhood Education,* 3 (2), 109-118.

Perry, G. (1977). *Cross-cultural study on the effect of space and teacher controlling behavior.* ED 131 351.

Perry, G. (1990). Alternate models of teacher preparation. In C. Seefeldt (Ed.), *Continuing issues in early childhood education.* Toronto: Merrill Publishing Company, 186-198.

Peters, D.L., & Sutton, R.E. (1984). The effects of CDA training on the beliefs, attitudes and behaviors of Head Start personnel. *Child Care Quarterly,* 13, 251-261.

Peterson, C., & Peterson, R. (1986). Parent-child interaction and day care: Does quality of day care matter? *Journal of Applied Developmental Psychology,* 7, 1-15.

Phillips, D., & Howes, C. (1987). Indicators of quality in child care: A review of the research. In D. Phillips (Ed.), *Quality in child care: What does the research tell us?* Washington, D.C: National Association for the Education of Young Children, 1-19.

Phillips, D., Howes, C., & Whitebook, M. (1991). Child care as an adult work environment. *Journal of Social Issues,* 47(2), 49-70.

Phillips, D., Howes, C., & Whitebook, M. (1992). The social policy context of child care: Effects on quality. *American Journal of Community Psychology,* 20(1), 25-51.

Phillips, D., McCartney, K., & Scarr, S. (1987). Child-care quality and children's social development. *Developmental Psychology,* 23(4), 537-543.

Phyfe-Perkins, E. (1979). *Children's behavior in preschool settings: A review of research concerning the influence of the physical environment.* Paper presented at the annual meeting of the American Educational Research Foundation, San Francisco, California. ED 168 722.

Piaget, J. (1950). *The psychology of intelligence.* London, England: Routledge & Kegan Paul.

Piaget, J. (1972). *Science of education and the psychology of the child* (revised edition). New York: Viking.

Pickering, L.K., Evans, D.G., Dupont, H.L., Vottet, J.J., & Evans, D.J. (1981). Diarrhea caused by Shigella, Rotavirus, and Giardia in day care centres: Prospective study. *Journal of Pediatrics,* 99, 51-56.

Pickering, L.K., & Woodward, W.E. (1982). Diarrhea in day care centers. *Pediatric Infectious Diseases*, 1, 47-52.

Powell, D.R. (1977). *Day care and the family: A study of interactions and congruency.* Lafayette, Indiana: Perdue University. ED 143 430.

Powell, D.R. (1980). Toward a socioecological perspective of relations between parents and child care programs. In S. Kilmer (Ed.), *Advances in early education and day care,* Vol. I. Grenwich, Conn: JAI Press, 203-226.

Powell, D.R. (1989). *Families and early childhood programs.* Washington, D.C: National Association for the Education of Young Children.

Powell, D.R., & Dunn, L. (1990). Non-baccalaureate teacher education in early childhood education. In B. Spodek & O.N. Saracho (Eds.), *Early childhood teacher preparation: Yearbook in early childhood education,* Vol. 1. New York: Teachers College Press, Columbia University, 45-66.

Prescott, E. (1981). Relations between physical setting and adult/child behavior in day care. In S. Kilmer (Ed.), *Advances in early education and day care,* Vol. II. Grenwich, Conn: JAI Press, 129- 158.

Prescott, E., Jones, E., & Krititchevsky, S. (1967). *Group child care as a child rearing environment.* Final report to the Children's Bureau. Pasadena, California: Pacific Oaks College. ED 062 014.

Quilitch, H.R., & Risely, T.R. (1973). The effects of play materials on social play. *Journal of Applied Behavior Analysis*, 6(4), 573-578.

Ramey, C.T., & Haskins, R. (1981). The modification of intelligence through early experience. *Intelligence*, 5, 5-9.

Ramsey, P. (1987). *Teaching and learning in a diverse world: Multicultural education for young children.* New York: Teachers College Press.

Rohe, W., & Nuffer, E.L. (1977). *The effects of density and partitioning on children's behavior.* Paper presented at the annual meeting of the American Psychological Association. San Francisco, California. ED 144 721.

Rosenthall, M.K. (1991). Behaviors and beliefs of caregivers in family day care. *Early Childhood Research Quarterly*, 6(2), 263-283.

Rothstein-Fisch, C., & Howes, C. (1988). Toddler peer interaction in mixed-age groups. *Journal of Applied Developmental Psychology*, 9, 211-218.

Rubenstein, J., and Howes, C. (1979). Caregiver and infant behavior in day care and in homes, *Developmental Psychology*, 15(1), 1-24.

Rubenstein, J., & Howes, C. (1983). Adaptation to infant day care. In S. Kilmer (Ed.), *Advances in early education and day care,* Vol. III. Grenwich, Conn: JAI Press, 13-45.

Rule, S., Killoran, J., Stowitschek, J., Innocenti, M., & Striefel, S. (1985). Training and support for mainstreaming day care staff. *Early Child Development and Care*, 20, 99-113.

Ruopp, R., Travers, J., Glantz, R., & Coelen, C. (1979). *Children at the center.* Final report of the National Day Care Study. Cambridge, Mass: Abt Associates.

Saltz, R., & Boesen, C. (1985). *Effects of a university CDA teacher education program: Findings of a three-year study.* Dearborn, Michigan: University of Michigan at Dearborn. ED 264 018.

Schliecker, E., White, D.R., & Jacobs, E. (1991). The role of day care quality in the prediction of children's vocabulary. *Canadian Journal of Behavioral Science*, 23(1), 12-24.

Schom-Moffat, P. (1984). *The bottom line: Wages and working conditions of workers in the formal day care market.* Submitted to the Task Force on Child Care. Ottawa, Ontario: Minister of Supplies and Services.

Schwarz, J.C. (1983). *Infant day care: effects at 2,4, and 8 years.* Paper presented at the biennial meeting of the Society for Research in Child Development. Detroit, Michigan. ED 233 806.

Schweinhart, L.J., Weikart, D.P., & Larner, M.B. (1986). Consequences of three preschool curriculum models through age 15. *Early Childhood Research Quarterly,* 1(1), 15-45.

Shapiro, S. (1975). Preschool ecology: A study of 3 environmental variables. *Reading Improvement,* 12, 236-341.

Silva, R.J. (1980). Hepatitis and the need for adequate standards in federally supported day care. *Child Welfare,* 59(7), 387-400.

Smith, A.B., & Hubbard, P.M. (1988). The relationship between parent/staff communication and children's behavior in early childhood settings. *Early Child Development and Care,* 35, 13-28.

Smith, A.B., McMillan, B.W., Kennedy, S., & Ratcliffe, B. (1989). The effect of improving preschool teacher/child ratios: An experiment in nature, *Early Child Development and Care,* 41, 123-138.

Smith, C., & Greenberg, M. (1981). Step by step integration of handicapped preschool children in a day care center for nonhandicapped children. *Journal of the Division for Early Childhood,* 2, 96-101.

Smith, P.K., & Connolly, K.J. (1980). *The ecology of preschool behaviour.* Cambridge, England: Cambridge University Press.

Smith, P.K., & Connolly, K.J. (1986). Experimental studies of the preschool environment: The Sheffield Project. In S. Kilmer (Ed.), *Advances in early education and day care,* Vol. IV. Grenwich, Conn: JAI Press, 27-67.

Snider, M.H., & Fu, V.R. (1990). The effects of specialized education and job experience on early childhood teachers' knowledge of developmentally appropriate practice. *Early Childhood Research Quarterly,* 5(1), 69-78.

SPR Associates (1986). *An exploratory review of selected issues in for-profit versus not-for-profit child care.* Paper prepared for the Special Committee on Child Care, Toronto, Ontario. Toronto, Ontario: Author.

Stith, S.M., & Davis, A.J. (1984). Employed mothers and family day care substitute care-givers: A comparitive analysis of infant care. *Child Development,* 55(4), 1340-1348.

Stoneman, Z. (1993). The effects of attitude on preschool integration. In C.A. Peck, S.L. Odom, & D.D. Bricker (Eds.), *Integrating young children with disabilities into community programs.* Baltimore, MA: Paul Brookes Publishing Co., 223-248.

Strain, P.S. (1984). Social behavior patterns of nonhandicapped and nonhandicapped developmentally disabled friend peers in mainstreamed schools. *Analysis and Intervention in Developmental Disabilities,* 3, 23-34.

Strain, P.S. (1990). LRE for preschool children with handicaps: What we know, what we should be doing. *Journal of Early Intervention,* 14, 291-296.

Stremmel, A.J. (1991). Predictors of intention to leave child care work. *Early Childhood Research Quarterly,* 6, 285-298.

Striefel, S., Killoran, J., & Quintero, M. (1991). *Functional integration for success: Preschool intervention.* Austin, Texas: Pro-ed.

Stuart, B., & Pepper, S. (1988). The contribution of the caregiver's personality and vocational interests to quality in licensed family day care. *Canadian Journal of Research in Early Childhood Education*, 2(2), 99-109.

Sundell, K. (1993). *Mixed age groups in Swedish nursery school and compulsory school.* Paper presented at the Third European Conference on the Quality of Early Childhood Education. Thesolonika, Greece.

Swick, K.J., & McKnight, S. (1989). Characteristics of kindergarten teachers who promote parent involvement. *Early Childhood Research Quarterly*, 4(1), 19-29.

Sylva, K., Roy, C., & Painter, H. (1980). *Childwatching at play group and nursery school.* London, England: Grant McIntyre.

Templeman, T.P., Fredericks, H.D.B., & Udell, T. (1989). Integration of children with moderate and severe handicaps into a day care center. *Journal of Early Intervention*, 13, 315-328.

Tzelepis, A., Giblin, P.T., & Agronow, S.J. (1983). Effects of adult caregiver's behaviors on the activities, social interactions, and investments of nascent preschool day care groups. *Journal of Applied Developmental Psychology*, 4, 201-216.

Ungaretti, T. (1987). *The relationship between family day care providers' participation in a college training program and the quality of the child care.* Unpublished paper, quoted in Kontos (1992).

Vandell, D.L., & Corasaniti, M.A. (1990). Variations in early child care: Do they predict subsequent social, emotional, and cognitive differences? *Early Childhood Research Quarterly*, 5, 555-572.

Vandell, D.L., Henderson, V.K., & Wilson, K.S. (1988). A longitudinal study of children with day care experiences of varying quality. *Child Development*, 59, 1286-1292.

Vandell, D.L., & Powers, C.P. (1983). Day care quality and children's free play activities. *American Journal of Orthopsychiatry*, 53(3), 493-500.

Vygotsky, L. (1978). *Mind, self, and society.* Chicago: University of Chicago Press.

Warren, S.F., & Kaiser, A.P. (1988). Research in early language intervention. In S.L. Odom & M.B. Karnes (Eds.), *Early intervention for infants and children with handicaps.* Baltimore, MA: Paul Brookes Publishing Co., 89-108.

West, S. (1988). *A study on compliance with the Day Nurseries Act at full-day child care centres in Metropolitan Toronto.* Prepared for the Toronto Area Office, Ontario Ministry of Community and Social Services. Toronto, Ontario: Ontario Ministry of Community and Social Services.

White, D. (1989). *Day care quality and the transition to kindergarten: What we can learn from research on children in day care settings.* Paper presented to the National Day Care Conference. Winnipeg, Manitoba.

White, D.R., Jacobs, E.V., & Schliecker, E. (1988). Relationship of day care environment quality and children's social behaviour. *Canadian Psychology*, 29, Abstract No. 668.

White, D.R., Parent, M.B., Chang, H., & Spindler, J. (1992). Parental selection of quality child care. *Canadian Journal of Research in Early Childhood Education*, 3(2), 101-108.

Whitebook, M., Howes, C., Darrah, R., & Friedman, J. (1982). Caring for the caregivers: Staff burnout in child care. In L. Katz (Ed.), *Current topics in early childhood education*, Vol. IV. Norwood, New Jersey: Ablex, 211-235.

Whitebook, M., Howes, C., & Phillips, D. (1989). *Who cares? Child care teachers and the quality of care in America. Executive Summary of the National Child Care Staffing Study.* Oakland, California: Child Care Employee Project.

Whitebook, M., Howes, C., & Phillips, D. (1990). *Who cares? Child care teachers and the quality of care in America. Final Report of the National Child Care Staffing Study.* Oakland, California: Child Care Employee Project.

Winget, M., Winget, W.G., & Popplewell, J.F. (1982). Including parents in evaluating family day care homes, *Child Welfare*, 61(4), 195-205.

Wolery, M., Strain, P.S., & Bailey, D.B. Jr. (1992). Reaching potentials of children with special needs. In S. Bredekamp & T. Rosegrant (Eds.), *Reaching potentials: Appropriate curriculum and assessment for young children*, Volume I. Washington, DC: National Association for the Education of Young Children.

Wright, M. (1983). *Compensatory education in the preschool: A Canadian approach.* Ypsilanti, Michigan: High Scope Press.

Yoshida, M.A., & Davies, M.E. (1982). Parenting in a new culture: Experiences of East Indian, Portuguese, and Caribbean mothers, *Multiculturalism*, 5(3), 3-5.

Index

A

Abusiveness, 90
Academy of Early Childhood
    Programs
        recommended staff-to-child
        ratios, 168
Accreditation, 113-114
Administration, 89-90
Age-appropriate behavior, 26, 34
    and staff behavior, 26, 34
    and staff education, 81
Aggression, 34
    effect of age difference on,
    171, 172
    and staff-to-child ratios, 71
Aimless wandering
    and adult detachment, 40
    connection to staff turnover,
    92
    definition of, 27
    and density, 78
    and harshness, 41
American Academy of
    Pediatrics
        provisions for health and
        safety, 67
American National Child Care
    Staffing Study
        on working conditions, 87, 88
American National Day Care Study
    on effect of group size, 73
Anti-bias programming, 132. *See
    also* Bias
Association for Childhood
    Education International, 32
Association for the Education of
    Young Children, 32
Auspices, 102-106
Autism, 137. *See also* Disabilities;
    Special needs

B

Behavior
    adult
        discrete, 25
        effect of group size on,
        73-75

        effect of staff-to-child
        ratio on, 68, 70, 71, 72
        and home-based child
        care, 63
        impact of credentialing
        on, 114
        impact of job satisfac-
        tion on, 90
        negative types, 38-42.
        See also Detachment;
        Restrictiveness;
        Harshness
        and program size, 76
        research into, 162
        See also Behaviors, adult
age-appropriate, 26, 34, 81,
135, 137, 140
child, 71, 75, 76, 154-156, 172
discriminatory, 123-126
settings, 60, 62. *See also*
    Environment, physical
Behaviors, adult, 22, 24, 37, 176
    identifying, 3
    positive types of
        developmentally
        appropriate, 32-34
        positive interaction,
        28-30
        responsiveness, 25-28
        verbal exchange, 32-34
    predictors of, 34-37, 42-45.
    See also Education; Work
    environment
    study of, 152, 154-156
Bias, 120
    addressing, 122
    anti-bias, 132
    cultural bias, 122
    in research, 154
    societal, 121
    teaching, 123

C

Canadian Child Care Federation
    on staff-to-child ratios, 70,
    72, 168
Canadian Paediatric Society
    recommendations for health
    and safety, 67. *See also*
    Health and safety
Center-based child care
    group size in, 73-74, 75

impact of staff education on,
    79, 80-81. *See also* Education
    physical environment of,
    60-61
    positive interaction in, 29
    regulation of, 98
    responsiveness in, 27
    and staff-to-child ratios, 70
    and verbal exchanges, 31
Center size, 76, 77
Child care programs
    center-based, 2, 20. *See also*
    Center-based
    credentialing and, 114
    defined, 2-3
    home-based, 2, 20. *See also*
    Home-based child care
    non-profit, 102, 106
    non-relative, 10
    school-age programs, 2, 31
Child Development Associate, 114
Child rearing practices, 48, 130
Children
    daily experience of, 22
    native, 162
    special needs, 134-146
Cognitive development, 27, 32,
    34, 171
    and Piaget, 45. *See also* Piaget
    and staff-to-child ratios, 70
Cognitive skills, 33, 61
    effect of mixed-age groups
    on, 174
    effect of socioeconomic
    status on, 176
    effect of staff education on,
    82
    and mainstreaming, 138
    research into, 163
    and special needs, 135, 137
Communication
    between children, 171
    between staff and children,
    30, 31
    between staff and parents,
    49, 50, 110
    patterns in child care, 166
    skills, 72, 137, 138
Concurrent
    enrollment, 166-167
    research, 16-19, 159
Consistency, staff, 48, 53-57
    and special needs child, 146

Consultation, 147. *See also*
  Transdisciplinary approach
Credentialing, 114-115
Cultural biases, 122
Cultural diversity, 7, 50
  and child rearing, 130
  children's awareness of,
  120-121, 128
  and family involvement, 146
  impact of research on, 161
  and programming, 58
  and standardized tests, 157
Curriculum. *See* Programming
Custodial program, 3

D

Day care center, 2
Density
  impact on behavior, 77-78
Detachment, staff, 39-40, 45, 70
Development, 7, 72
  cognitive, 171. *See also*
  Cognitive skills
  and disabilities, 137, 149
  effect of for-profit child care
  on, 103
  effect of program on, 176
  effect of socioeconomic
  status on, 176
  and mainstreaming, 138
  and self-concept, 149
  social, 171. *See also* Social
  skills
Developmental gains
  for special needs child care,
  145
Developmental psychology, 160,
  163
Developmentally appropriate
  activities, 68-69, 73-74, 79,
  87, 89, 104, 112
Developmentally appropriate
  practice, 32-34, 35, 36, 58,
  81, 84
  and age-differences, 171
  and special needs child care,
  142, 150
Developmentally appropriate programming, 147, 168-170.
  See also Programming
Disabilities
  child comfort with, 139
  child reaction to, 143

cultural perspective on, 146
developmental, 137
and the physical environ-
  ment, 149
training for, 142
Discrete
  behaviors, 25, 38-42
  perspective, 15
Division for Early Childhood of
  the Council for Exceptional
  Children, 145, 146, 149
Down Syndrome, 138, 142. *See
  also* Special-needs child care

E

Early childhood centers, 2
Early childhood education, 167.
  See also Education
Early childhood education, 3, 13,
  83, 167. *See also* Education;
  Training
Early Childhood Environmental
  Rating Scale, 16, 19, 68, 71,
  75, 98
  as a self-review tool, 115
  and work environment, 88, 89
Early childhood programs,
  1, 11, 50
Education
  and age-appropriateness, 168
  association with adult
  behavior, 97
  in early childhood programming, 35, 42-43, 45, 167
  parent, 116
  public, 116-117
  staff, 37, 104, 110, 116
Enforcement
  of regulations, 97. *See also*
  Regulations
Environment
  administrative, 13
  home, 12
  physical, 12, 13, 59-63, 126-
  127, 134, 149. *See also*
  Physical environment
  preparation of, 58
  safety, 45.
  See also Health and safety
  structural features, 22
  working, 22, 44-45, 87-93, 95,
  104. *See also* Working
  environment

Environment Rating Scale, 102
Environmental risk, 9, 112
Equipment
  need for, 78
Ethnicity, 123, 128, 130, 131, 149,
  162
Exploration
  child, 33, 54. *See also* Piaget

F

Family Day Care Rating Scale,
  81, 99
Family
  involvement in programs,
  130-132, 146
  stress, 175. *See also* Stress
For-profit child care, 102-106
Funding, 95-96, 102

G

Gender difference, 132
Global
  measure of quality, 91-92,
  101, 118
  perspective, 11, 15-16, 24, 25
Government regulation, 112. *See
  also* Regulatory methods
Group sizes, 13, 73-76, 110, 167

H

Harshness, 41-42, 45, 72
Health and safety, 3, 13, 66-68,
  77, 101
Home-based child care, 27-28, 29-
  30, 31, 61, 63, 118
  and group size, 76
  impact of staff education on,
  78-80, 81, 82
  regulation in, 99
  and safety, 44
  sponsorship in, 100
  and staff-to-child ratios, 71
Home environment, 12
Hygiene practices, 57, 67. *See also*
  Health and safety

mechanisms for obtaining, 110-118. *See also* Regulatory methods; Professional practices
and non-profit child care, 106
and parental involvement, 51
and regulation, 99
requirements for, 13. *See also* Education; Environment; Group sizes; Health and safety; Programming; Staff-to-child ratios; Staffing; Training

R

Racial identity, 131. *See also* Cultural diversity
Ratio. *See* Staff-to-child ratio
Regulation, 96-99
Regulatory methods, 110, 112-113
Research methods
methodological difficulties, 160-164
types
concurrent, 16, 159
discrete, 15
global, 11, 15, 24
interviews and questionnaires, 157-158
laboratory experiments, 152-154
longitudinal, 11, 16, 160
naturalistic observation, 154-156
standardized tests, 157
Responsiveness, 25-28, 54, 74, 84, 142
impact of staff-to-child ratios on, 36
Restrictiveness, 40-41, 45
effect of group size on, 74
effect of program size on, 77
impact of staff-to-child ratio on, 70, 72

S

Safety. *See* Health and safety
Salaries. *See* Staff salaries
School-age programs, 2

School-based programs, 31, 60-61, 79
Secure attachments, 27, 53-54
Segregated programs, 135, 138
Self-concept, child, 121-122, 144, 149
Self-confidence, child, 130
Self-esteem, child, 170
Self-review, 115
Skill development, 3, 57
Skills
age-appropriate, 140, 141
cognitive, 33, 61, 82, 135, 137, 138, 163, 174, 176
communication, 8, 138, 172
intellectual, 9-10
language, 8-9, 12, 31, 82, 135, 141, 174, 176
social, 8, 12, 24, 30, 31, 61, 135, 137, 138, 140, 163, 174
Social
competence, 31, 77, 80
development, 32, 171
environments, 6
games, 32
interaction, 137
needs, 135
skills. *See* Skills, social
stimulation, 74, 81
Socioeconomic status, 9, 161, 162, 164, 175-176
Special needs child care, 134, 138, 145, 146
and civil rights, 135
staff education for, 82
Sponsorship, impact of, 101
Staff
communication with parents, 110
consistency, 53-57
education, 78-84, 104. *See also* Education; Training
qualifications, 4
salaries, 87, 92, 95, 96, 110
training, 16, 67, 138, 142, 166, 167, 173
turnover rates, 6, 22, 53, 54, 56, 57, 87, 91-92, 96, 105
Staff-to-child ratios, 4, 13, 20, 22, 35-36, 43, 68-72, 110, 167, 168
and group size, 73
in non-profit centers, 103, 104
public education about, 116

and the work environment, 88
Statistically significant defined, 164
Statistically significant relationship defined, 27
Stress
in children, 78, 169
in the family, 175
job related, 72

T

Tests, standardized, 157, 163, 164
Training, 19, 35, 138, 166
in child development, 13
and credentialing, 114
in early childhood education, 13
in health, 67
in-service, 117
for mixed-ages, 173
of parents, 50
and professional development, 37
in safety, 67
for special needs child care, 142
Transdisciplinary approach, 143, 147-149, 150
Turnover, staff, 6, 22, 53, 54, 56, 57, 87, 91-92, 96, 105

V

Verbal
development, 70, 84
exchange, 30-31, 36, 76

W

Work environment, 22, 87-93, 95, 104-105. *See also* Administration; Job satisfaction; Preparation time; Salaries; Staff-to-child ratios; Staff turnover

Z

Zone of proximal growth, 171, 174